GUEST

GUEST
A CHANGELING TALE

MARY DOWNING HAHN

SCHOLASTIC INC.

No part of this publication may be reproduced, stored in a retrieval system, or transmitted in any form or by any means, electronic, mechanical, photocopying, recording, or otherwise, without written permission of the publisher. For information regarding permission, write to Clarion Books, a Houghton Mifflin Harcourt Publishing Company imprint, 3 Park Avenue, 19th Floor, New York, NY 10016.

ISBN 978-1-338-65917-7

Copyright © 2019 by Mary Downing Hahn. All rights reserved. Published by Scholastic Inc., 557 Broadway, New York, NY 10012, by arrangement with Clarion Books, a Houghton Mifflin Harcourt Publishing Company imprint. SCHOLASTIC and associated logos are trademarks and/or registered trademarks of Scholastic Inc.

The publisher does not have any control over and does not assume any responsibility for author or third-party websites or their content.

12 11 10 9 8 7 6 5 4 3 2 1 20 21 22 23 24 25

Printed in the U.S.A. 40

First Scholastic printing, January 2020

The text was set in Palatino LT Std.

For Collin and Joseph

1

I WAS IN A TEMPER fit to blow the lid off a kettle of boiling water. And who wouldn't be? Since sunup, I'd been doing chores. I'd milked the cow, hauled two buckets of water from the well, fed the chickens, and then fought the hens for their eggs. Now I was down on my knees, sweat-soaked and bug-bitten, yanking weeds from the vegetable patch. My hands were caked with mud, and my nose was burned as red as a strawberry. Midges hummed around my face and bit my ears.

Wiping the sweat from my eyes, I yanked a thistle out by its roots, only to see two more hiding in the beans. I scowled at my baby brother, Thomas, who lay nearby on the grass.

"You," I muttered. "If it weren't for you, I'd be down the lane, skipping rope with the village girls. But, oh no, I must watch you and do chores as if I were a servant. You've ruined my life, that's what you've done. It's a wicked thing to say, but sometimes I wish you'd never been born!"

Thomas smiled at me and cooed as if I'd praised him. Ashamed, I clapped my hand over my mouth and hoped Mam hadn't heard me, but she was in the cottage, singing at her loom, weaving soft blankets to keep Thomas warm when winter came.

I watched Thomas playing with his toes and chuckling to himself. Truth to tell, he was a sweet baby. I'd be lying if I said he wasn't. He never fussed, never cried, he ate what he was fed, and slept the whole night through.

And he was beautiful, even though no one said so. When visitors came, they leaned over the cradle and frowned and scowled and shook their heads.

"'Tis a pity he's so ugly and puny," they'd say.

"Oh yes, he's a sickly one. He'll not live past his first year."

"And such a nasty temper he's got."

"No good will come of him."

"If I caught a fish half as ugly as that poor babby, I'd throw it back."

It was as if each visitor tried to come up with a worse insult than the one before.

And all the while, Mam and Dadoe and I smiled and nodded in agreement, for all of us, even the youngest, knew it was bad luck to compliment a baby. Since the day my brother was born, I'd been warned not to speak of his pretty curls or his blue eyes or his dimples. I mustn't boast of his sweet nature or praise him in any way.

It was the Kinde Folke we feared. Although no one in our village had seen them for many a year, they could be far away or just outside the cottage door. They were sly and full of tricks, and no matter what we called them, they were far from kind, though no one ever dared say that aloud either. If we spoke of them at all, it was to say they were wise, they were beautiful, they were brave and noble and honest in their dealings.

When in truth, if we offended them, they burned our barns and cottages, stole our livestock, sent plagues to sicken us, cursed our fields with thistles, lamed our horses, and dried up our cows' milk.

Worst of all, if the Kinde Folke learned of a beautiful baby boy's birth, they'd steal him away and leave one of their own sickly creatures in his place. And what misery the changeling would bring to its new mother. As if it weren't bad enough that her own sweet baby was gone, changelings screamed and cried and bit and pinched and broke things. She'd have no rest, that poor mother, no joy.

And so we did our best to keep Thomas safe. I watched him while Mam did her housework, and she and Dadoe watched him at night. We never even whispered sweet things to him for fear the Kinde Folke would come for him.

Their spies were everywhere. Long-eared rabbits listened in the hedges, and sharp-eyed crows watched from chimney tops. Toads in ponds, fish in streams, foxes slinking by, any and all might carry messages to the Kinde Folke.

I stabbed my trowel into the dirt and dug out a stubborn thistle. I shouldn't have spoken so crossly to Thomas. He was too young to understand my words, but he must have heard the anger in my voice.

A crow cawed, and I looked up to see him perched in a tree over my head. He ruffled his black wings and stared down at me. His dark eye reflected a sliver of light. Keeping watch on me, he cawed again. It sounded as if he were laughing at me.

Suddenly anxious, I glanced at Thomas. He'd just learned to sit up, and he was looking at me to make sure I'd noticed. The small chain he always wore around his neck lay in the grass. Its silver locket sparkled in the sunlight.

Dropping the trowel, I ran to fetch the locket. "Old Granny Hedgepath gave you this, Thomas. You're not to take it off.

You'd best do what that old witch says, or she'll eat you for dinner."

Thomas laughed and clapped his hands. What did he know of witches and their ways?

I tried to slip the necklace over his head, but he grabbed the chain and held it out for me to take. Giving things to people was his new game. Most people, including me, gave them back, but Matthew down the lane had run home with the wooden cow Dadoe had carved for Thomas. I'd gone to his house and asked him for it.

"Babby give it me," Matthew wailed. Luckily for Thomas, but not for Matthew, his mam snatched the toy cow, handed it to me, and gave Matthew a smack.

I took the chain from Thomas and smiled. Without thinking, I said, "Oh, Thomas, you're so sweet. How could I ever be vexed with you? You're the best baby in the world. And the prettiest."

When I tried again to slip the chain over his head, he ducked away laughing.

I held the necklace out, but instead of continuing the struggle, I sat in the grass and admired the necklace. The silver chain was finely made, and the heart-shaped locket was decorated all over with a cunning pattern of vines and flowers. I sighed. It was much too pretty to waste on a boy.

In truth, I'd wanted the locket from the day Granny Hedgepath fastened the chain around my brother's neck. "Make sure Thomas wears this always," she'd told Mam. "Never remove it. He must eat and sleep with it around his neck. Even when you bathe him, make sure the locket stays fastened. It will protect him from mischief."

Placing her bony hand on Thomas's head, Granny added, "May the Kinde Folke of the forest find joy elsewhere and ignore this poor ugly baby."

I was watching Granny from my shadowy corner, neither moving nor speaking. It frightened me to look at her, but she drew my eyes like the evil cockatrice. Her white hair was wild and uncombed. Sticks and leaves poked out of its tangles. She had long yellow fingernails, as sharp as a hawk's talons, and her eyes were sunken so deep in their sockets, I couldn't tell their color.

Some said the old woman was a healer, others said she was a witch, but everyone in the village agreed she knew magic and spells and walked in Mirkwood at midnight. They also knew not to anger her.

Suddenly Granny turned to me in my corner. "Why are you sulking there, girl? I see your sly eyes, I hear the beat of your jealous heart. The necklace is for your brother. You have no need for it."

She spoke as if I were a wicked girl, a bad sister, someone not to be trusted. Even though it was rude, I turned my head away and scowled at the floor. How had Granny guessed I wanted that necklace? It belonged around my neck, not my brother's.

After Granny left, Mam said, "You shamed me, Mollie. I've taught you to smile and curtsy when you see Granny Hedgepath, but you did neither. What must she think of you?"

"I don't care what she thinks. Did you not hear what she said to me? She was hateful and rude."

"No, it was you who was hateful and rude." Mam looked at me. "I hope you haven't made an enemy of that old woman."

"I don't care if I have. I'm not afraid of her." If Mam had had Granny's skill, she'd have known I was indeed scared of the old woman. I knew full well I should have been polite, but my tongue had a way of getting away from me. I said what I thought and didn't think about the consequences until it was too late.

Now, far from Granny's prying eyes, I held the necklace up and watched it sparkle in the sunlight. "You want me to wear this, don't you?" I asked Thomas. "That's why you gave it to me."

He smiled so widely, I saw the buds of new teeth pushing up through his pink gums. Surely Thomas wouldn't come to harm if I wore the necklace for just a few moments. With care I undid the clasp and fastened the chain around my neck. How beautiful it was.

I should have given the necklace back to Thomas, but instead I tucked it inside my dress. I liked the smooth feel of the locket against my skin. Just for a little while, I thought. What harm could come to Thomas with me so near?

It seemed at least a dozen thistles had sprouted while my back was turned. Their thorny stems hurt my hands, and their roots held the soil tightly. I tugged and tugged until my back hurt from bending over. If I did much more weeding, I'd be an old woman before I even grew up. I'd hobble around in ragged clothes and end up as crazy as Granny Hedgepath.

While I worked, a large cloud drifted across the sun and plunged the garden into its shadow. At the same time, the breeze dropped and a strange silence fell. No leaves rustled.

Chickens stopped clucking and disappeared into their coop. No birds sang. No bees hummed in the clover. The colors of flowers and grass, trees and sky faded to gray.

Worried, I got to my feet to check on Thomas. Suddenly the world seemed to spin and lurch. Colors blurred and ran together. I saw two of everything. The sky was beneath me, the grass above me. Too dizzy to stand, I fell to the ground. The last thing I heard was a crow laughing.

2

When I opened my eyes, I was lying flat on my back in the garden. I got to my feet slowly, lightheaded from the heat and as weak-legged as if I'd run to the top of Cat Tail Hill and down the other side.

The cloud was gone, and the sun shone. Hens pecked in the dirt; a robin sang from its perch on a fence post; bees buzzed. A cool breeze blew through the leaves. The crow had left its perch.

My brother was just as I'd left him, sound asleep on the quilt. Bending over him, I tickled the sole of his foot to wake him, but instead of laughing and stretching out his arms to be picked up, he began to cry. His face turned an ugly shade of red. His screams sounded more like a cat than a baby. When I tried to lift him, he kicked and hit me.

Pulling the locket out of my dress, I offered it to him, but he screamed at its touch.

"Thomas!" I cried. "Thomas, it's me—Mollie. What's wrong? Why are you crying?"

Thomas ignored me and continued to scream and kick. After a struggle, I finally got a grip on the squirming baby and carried him, shrieking with rage, into the cottage.

Mam ran to meet us. "Whatever's the matter with Thomas? Is he bee-stung? Spider-bit?"

When she tried to take him in her arms, he fought her just as he'd fought me. He screeched and howled as if he'd never stop.

"Quick, Mollie," Mam said, "fill a tub with cool water. He's suffering from the heat."

On shaky legs, I ran to the well and drew a pail of water. Mam hadn't noticed that Thomas wasn't wearing the necklace. I'd put it around his neck later when he'd calmed down and no one was looking.

While I filled the tub, Mam stripped Thomas of his clothing and plunged him into the water. For a moment, the surprise silenced him. Mam examined him but found no sign of sting or bite. Soon he began to scream again.

Mam wrapped him in a soft blanket and rocked him in

her arms. Nothing she did calmed him. If anything, Thomas screamed louder.

"Fetch Granny Hedgepath, Mollie!" Mam cried. "Make haste!"

Full of fear and dread, I ran into the lane, up Cat Tail Hill, and down the other side. Behind me was Thomas, perhaps dead already, and before me was Granny Hedgepath. Only out of love for Thomas would I go to her door and knock.

"What do you want, girl?" The old woman's voice was as harsh and as merciless as the crow's. "Can't I have a moment's peace without some fool child hammering at my door?"

"Please, Granny, it's Thomas," I said, gasping. "He's screaming like a banshee and won't let Mam or me touch him. Mam sent me to fetch you. Can you please come? He's only a wee baby."

"Tush. Most likely it's nothing more than a spider bite or a bee sting."

She began to close the door, but I cried, "Mam already looked him over. There's not a mark on him. Thomas never cries, he's the best—"

"Oh, fie, girl, shut your mouth. You never know who's

listening, do you?" Granny Hedgepath frowned, but she hobbled inside to get her medicine bag.

From the open door, I saw an old table and a spindly chair. Dried herbs dangled in bunches from the rafters. The rest of the cottage hid in shadows, which seemed unnaturally thick in the corners.

Granny stepped outside as quiet as a mouse in a room full of cats. Scowling and muttering to herself, she pinched my arm. "Come along, come along, Sam Cloverall's girl. You'll see nothing in my cottage but what I want you to see."

I ran beside the old woman to keep up with her long strides. Although I spoke not a word, Granny continued to mumble and mutter. It was clear she disliked me, but what did it matter? I'd come to her to get help for Thomas. Once he was cured, I'd never visit her cottage. Whatever went on inside, I wanted nothing to do with any of it.

Long before we reached the gate, we heard Thomas screeching. "It's as if he's become 'pretend' Thomas," I said. "You know how we all say he's awful so they won't—"

Granny turned to me, her face fierce with anger. "Hush! Not another word from you, girl."

I covered my mouth with my hand to keep from saying something sassy and followed the old woman into our cottage.

Pushing Mam aside, Granny bent over Thomas. She poked and prodded; she looked; she even sniffed. Finally, she straightened up and stared Mam in the eye. "You must be brave and not flinch from what I'm about to tell you, Agnes Cloverall."

Mam trembled, and her breath came in gasps. "It's brain fever," she moaned. "Our Thomas will be dead before dawn."

"'Tis not brain fever. Indeed, 'tis far worse than that." Granny seized Mam's hand and held it tight. "This baby is not Thomas," she said. "They came for yours and left theirs in his place."

"No," Mam cried. "Look at him, of course he's our Thomas. Don't you think I know my own baby?"

Granny waved her hand in front of Mam's and my eyes. "Look again, Agnes Cloverall, and tell me what you see in that cradle."

Mam and I stared at the cradle. What lay there was long and scrawny, its face as wrinkled as an old man's and its eyes as yellow as a cat's. Tufts of hair finer than milkweed spores sprouted from his head. He glared at us, kicked his skinny legs, and howled like a wild thing.

Never had I seen a creature so ugly.

Mam screamed. "No, it cannot be. Oh, let it not be, Granny!"

I longed to take Mam's hand and comfort her, but I backed away in shame. This was my doing. I'd said what I shouldn't have said. I'd taken his necklace and worn it myself. If Mam learned what I'd done, she'd never forgive me. I pressed my hand to my chest and covered the tiny bump of the locket under my dress.

Mam turned to Granny, her eyes wild with fear and rage. "Get this creature out of my house," she cried. "It mustn't sully Thomas's cradle."

Granny took Mam's arm and forced her to look at the creature. "It's a hard thing I'm asking you, Agnes Cloverall, but you must keep him. Treat the changeling with kindness. Nurse him, sing to him, rock him as if he were your own sweet Thomas."

"Have you lost your wits?" Mam asked. "Nurse that creature? I can't, I won't. If you refuse to do it, I myself will take him to the crossroads tonight and leave him there. They can come for him or not. I want my own child, not this monster."

"Be still and listen." Granny's grip on Mam's arm tightened. "If you treat this changeling well, they'll treat Thomas well. But if you treat him badly, you can be sure your child's life with them will be filled with misery and suffering."

"If I mistreat this creature, they will mistreat Thomas?"

"That's their nature. They and theirs come first—even the ones they don't want. We and ours come last." She paused a moment. "If the changeling grows strong and healthy on human milk, they might take him and return yours. Mind you, it doesn't happen often, and I make no promises. There's a chance you'll get your Thomas back—but only if you please them."

Mam returned her gaze to the cradle. Tears ran down her face. "I do this not for you, but for Thomas," she told the changeling. "My own true child who's been taken from me."

With tears running down her face, she lifted the changeling to her breast and opened her dress. He began to suck at once. The only noise then was the sound of him nursing. Loud, slurping, as greedy as a piglet and many times uglier.

Granny Hedgepath steered me toward the door. "Leave your mam alone with it," she said. "She must have peace and quiet if she's to nurse the changeling."

She led me to a stone bench in the garden and sat beside

me. Thomas's quilt lay on the grass, rumpled and empty, a pitiful reminder of my little brother.

"It were you, weren't it? You said what you shouldn't have said." Granny Hedgepath held my arms tightly and forced me to face her. "Tell the truth—I'll know if you're lying, you wretched girl!"

Trembling with fear and guilt, I dared not confess to Granny. I tried to pull away, but the old woman's fingernails bit into my skin and I whimpered.

"Answer me!" Granny shook me so hard, my head bounced, as if the old woman meant to scramble my brains. "Careless, stupid girl, you praised Thomas, did you not? You boasted! You drew their attention."

"I didn't mean to speak out loud," I cried. "The words were supposed to stay in my head, but—"

The old woman shook me again. "I knew it the day I came with the locket and you hid in the shadows, sly as a snake. You were jealous of your brother. You *wanted* them to take him away!"

"No, no." I tried to escape the old woman's hold. "I love Thomas."

Granny Hedgepath shoved her face into mine so we were

nose to nose. Anger danced in her eyes. "I see the wickedness in you."

I turned my head away from Granny's face. Yes, I'd envied Thomas, but not enough to want the Kinde Folke to take him. No, surely I didn't. I wasn't that sort of sister.

If only the old woman would go away. I couldn't bear the strange earthy, smoky smell of her or the feel of her cloak, coarse and scratchy and old, against my skin. Her breath was raspy, and its odor was a mixture of herbs and spices and stale food. Once more I tried to free myself, but she didn't loosen her grip.

Suddenly she pulled the locket out of my dress and unfastened it, then held it in front of me. "So, you took the locket. I wondered why it hadn't kept the dear babby safe."

"Thomas gave it to me — he wanted me to have it. It was just for a little while. I meant to give it back, but, but . . ." I began to cry. The old woman was right. I was indeed a bad sister, a horrible sister, the worst sister a baby brother could ever have. "I didn't want them to take him, I didn't!"

She leaned even closer to me and hissed into my ear. "How do you like your *new* baby brother? Is he what you wanted?"

Without waiting for an answer, Granny Hedgepath hurled the necklace at me and strode toward the gate.

Shaking with anger, I shouted after her. "Don't you dare call that monster my brother!"

Granny Hedgepath looked back. "Best learn to mind your tongue, or it will forever bring you trouble."

With a swirl of her tattered cloak, the old woman strode through the gate and out of my sight.

Not knowing what else to do, I fastened the chain around my neck and hid the locket again under my dress. I was no longer comforted to feel it against my skin, but I didn't want anyone else to know I had it.

A few moments later, Dadoe came down the lane whistling, his work in the fields done for the day. Usually I ran to meet him. When I was little, he'd hoist me onto his shoulders and carry me home. How tall I'd felt perched up high. I could see over the green fields all the way to Mirkwood, lying like a dark shadow at the mountains' feet.

He'd laugh and say, "Shall I take you to Mirkwood and leave you there with the Kinde Folke?"

"No, Dadoe, no." I'd cling to him, terrified of that dark

wood and its mysteries. Never had I gone there, and never would I go.

This evening I didn't run to meet Dadoe. I sat on the bench and dreaded what he'd do when he saw the changeling in the cradle he'd made for Thomas.

Dadoe stopped in front of me. "Why, Mollie, what are you doing sitting here all by yourself without a word of greeting?"

A loud screeching in the cottage saved me from answering.

"That can't be our Thomas," Dadoe said, "wailing like a starving cat."

He looked at me as if he expected an answer. In a small voice, I said, "You're right, Dadoe, it's not our Thomas."

I'd spoken too low for Dadoe to hear. With a puzzled face, he went into the cottage, and I followed slowly.

Scooping up the changeling, he looked at Mam. "What's the matter with our Thomas? He looks a bit poorly."

Mam began to cry. I turned to Dadoe to explain, but before I opened my mouth to speak, Dadoe asked, "Has Granny Hedgepath seen him, Agnes? He looks worse than I first thought."

"Yes, yes, she's been here and gone," Mam sobbed. "There's nothing she can do."

"It must be bad if Granny can't help." Dadoe held the changeling close and rocked him gently. "Never fear, Thomas, we'll make you well again. There are other healers who know as much or more than Granny Hedgepath."

"Sam, are you blind?" Mam cried. "That's not Thomas in your arms!"

Dadoe smiled down at the changeling, who stared back with strange wide eyes. "Don't be daft," Dadoe said. "If he's not Thomas, who is he?" He laughed as if Mam were making a joke.

I snatched the changeling from Dadoe and held him in front of his face. "Look at him!" I screamed. "Can't you see this is not Thomas?"

Shrieking, the changeling wriggled and fought to escape, but I held him tightly. "They took Thomas today. And left *this* in his place."

Dadoe still did not see the truth. *"They?"*

"They," Mam said. "You know very well who Mollie means, Sam! Look at the baby properly."

Dadoe stared at the screaming creature in my arms. His face changed from worry about Thomas's health to horror at what he finally saw. "It cannot be," he whispered. "We've been so careful, Agnes. We've not said a word to draw them to our door."

Fearing he'd hurl the changeling at the wall, I took the strange baby from Dadoe. Shouting to make myself heard above the wailing, I said, "They came with their sickly baby and took our Thomas away with them."

Dadoe groaned and turned away from me. "We cannot keep their wicked creature."

"We must," Mam told him. "Granny Hedgepath says if we treat the changeling well, they'll treat Thomas well. If their sickly one thrives, they sometimes bring back the one they took and take their own away with them."

"They'll never bring our Thomas back," Dadoe said. "I'll carry their castoff to the crossroads this very night and leave him there for them to take or not."

"No." Mam took the wailing changeling from me. "We'll do as Granny Hedgepath says. We must, Sam—for Thomas's sake."

Dadoe watched her unfasten her dress and bring the changeling to her breast. "I cannot bear the sight of this." Without another word, he strode out of the cottage.

Mam ran to the door and called after him. "Where are you going, Sam?"

"To the tavern. There, I'll hear no screaming, yowling brat."

"When will you be home?" Mam cried.

"Not until you've taken that thing to the crossroads. I'll not sleep under this roof until it's gone." Dadoe opened the door and nearly ran from the cottage.

I put my arms around Mam and pressed my head against her side. Above me, the changeling kicked and squirmed and sucked Mam's milk as if he were starving.

"Dadoe will come back," I said, my heart breaking as I spoke. "He will, I know he will."

Mam pushed me away. "Leave me be, Mollie. I don't need you tugging at me too."

Gone was Mam's rosy face. Gone were her dimples, gone was her smile. From the worn, sad look of Mam, she might as well have been a changeling herself.

Late that night, I lay in my bed in the loft, hoping to hear Dadoe come home before I fell asleep, but the only sounds were the changeling's wails and shrieks and Mam's weary attempts to rock it to sleep. No footsteps in the lane, no sound at the door, no voice calling out Mam's name.

I felt the locket under my nightgown. I'd wear it forever, not because it was pretty but as a reminder of what I'd done.

3

Dadoe didn't come home that morning, nor the next, nor the one after that. A week passed without news of him. Finally, one of the local men told Mam that Dadoe had gone to a distant village and found a job there as a farm laborer. He wouldn't return until the changeling was gone—in one way or another, he said.

Even though it was my fault Dadoe had left, I was angry with him for abandoning Mam and me. Without Dadoe's wages, we had little to spend on flour and sugar. Mam grew too weak to do anything except care for the changeling, so I cooked and made sure Mam ate, but it seemed the changeling was sucking the life out of her.

While I milked the cow, weeded the garden, scrubbed the floor, and scoured pots, I wished the changeling would sicken and die. If I'd had the courage, I myself would have taken him to the crossroads while Mam slept.

As the changeling's belly grew round, he cried less, but still far more than a human baby. When he was angry or hungry, he bit and kicked and pulled Mam's hair. No matter how badly he behaved, Mam spoke softly and kindly to him. She rocked him and nursed him and gave him a name—Guest, for that's what he was, a guest in our home who would return to his people one day as Thomas would return to us.

Guest never smiled or laughed. He didn't gurgle or coo. When he wasn't crying, he lay in his cradle and scowled. Often he stared as cats do, at something only he could see.

I hoped it was the Kinde Folke he saw, coming and going in the cottage to make sure Mam treated their baby well. Surely they'd be pleased by his health. Someday soon they'd come with Thomas and trade him for Guest. Dadoe would return, and Mam would recover, and all would be as before.

A year passed, summer and fall and winter and spring, and still the Kinde Folke did not come. Guest outgrew the cradle, but he did not stand or walk. Not one word did he speak. Even though he'd grown a few tiny yellow teeth, he wanted only milk.

One morning, I stood at the garden gate with Guest in

my arms. Pointing across the green fields to Mirkwood, I said, "That's where your true people are, but they don't want you. Nobody wants you. Not even Mam. Certainly not me. You're a wicked, soulless creature, and I long to be rid of you forever."

It was wrong to say such things to Guest, but what did it matter? He understood nothing I said. He was more animal than human—a mongrel dog maybe, the runt of a litter who should have been drowned at birth.

Guest's yellow eyes gleamed, but what lay in the shadows behind them I couldn't guess. Most likely he hated me as much as I hated him.

Turning his head, he gazed across the fields to Mirkwood, a blue shadow in the distance, and made a series of strange harsh sounds.

"Listen to you," I said. "Click-clack, click-clack. Is that all you can say? A beast is what you are."

I felt a powerful urge to throttle him. To dash out his brains—if he had any. To drown him in the water trough. To leave him at the crossroads. Granny was wrong. No matter how we treated the changeling, the Kinde Ones would not bring Thomas back to us.

The sound of harness bells interrupted my thoughts. I

leaned over the gate and watched the peddler's horse come down the lane, pulling a cart heaped with the sorts of things you never knew you needed until you saw them, and then you couldn't forget them. Shiny new pots and pans, bolts of bright cloth, shoes and boots and hats, saws, hammers, barrels of nails, sacks of sugar, and smaller things like feathers, buttons, ribbons of all colors, spools of thread, combs, and pretty beads that sparkled in the sunlight.

The peddler sat on his high seat behind the horse and waved when he saw me. He'd known me since I was a baby and Mam and Dadoe long before that. If he had a name other than peddler, we'd never known it. But he came every month or so, and he knew the name of everyone in the village and on the farms.

He wore the same old blue coat, long and faded and patched here and there with bits of cloth that didn't match. On his head was a shapeless yellow hat with a crow's feather stuck in its band. A nose the size and shape of a carrot, but more red than orange, jutted from his face, and a bushy gray beard and drooping mustache hid his mouth.

Halting at our gate, the old man smiled down at me. "Here's pretty Mollie Cloverall, who needs silk ribbons for her hair, and perhaps a string of green beads to match her eyes, or maybe even a bouquet of flowers to give her mam."

Guest leaned toward the peddler and sniffed as if puzzled by his smell. I couldn't tell if he liked the smell or not. But it was the most interest Guest had shown in anything except milk.

The peddler laughed. "My, my, but you've got an ugly wee brother there, sniffing me more like a pup than a babby."

I scowled at the insult. Surely the peddler could see Guest was no relation to me. "He's not my brother."

"Well, now, if he's not your brother, who is he?"

Unwilling to admit what Guest was, I said, "A band of travelers left him in our garden."

The peddler scrutinized Guest, leaning so close, I thought he might sniff the changeling like a dog himself. "He don't look like a traveler's babby."

"Perhaps that's why they left him here." I was getting annoyed with the peddler's comments. "He's so ugly and mean and nasty, they didn't want him, and neither do I."

Guest turned his yellow eyes to me as he'd done before, and the old man said, "I believe he likes you more than you like him."

"He doesn't like anyone, and what's it to you, anyway?" In a huff, I walked into the cottage without looking back.

The peddler called after me, "Does this mean you won't be needing ribbons, beads, or flowers?"

My answer was to slam the door behind me. Dumping Guest in the cradle, I ran to the window and peeked out. All I saw of the peddler was his back as he drove away. I wanted the ribbons and the beads and the bouquet for Mam, but the peddler was entirely too nosy, him and his feather in his cap and his sly eyes. And, truth to tell, Mam had no coins to spare on frippery.

That afternoon, Granny Hedgepath came by. Before she crossed the threshold, I hid in the loft. I didn't want to see her or hear what she might say to me, but I did want to eavesdrop on what she said to Mam. I lay flat on the floor and pressed my ear to a knothole.

"I've brought more of my elixir to strengthen you," Granny said. "Is it helping you, Agnes?"

"All that will help me," Mam said, "is to hold Thomas in my arms again."

Granny mumbled something, and Mam said, "See how

this one has grown? Have I not been good to him? Have I not been kind?"

"You've been more than good and better than kind," Granny told her.

"Then tell me, why don't they come for him? My milk has put fat on his bones and taken it from my bones. He rarely cries now. He sleeps at night and wakes at dawn."

"But he doesn't talk or walk or even stand up like a proper young one. Why should they want him when they have yours?"

"But you said if I treated him well—"

"I said *perhaps*, Agnes Cloverall. *Perhaps* they'd take this one back and return yours."

Guest began to wail so loudly that I covered my ears.

"*Perhaps*," Mam hissed. "I've devoted myself to this creature for over a year, I've lost my husband and my strength, and you tell me *perhaps*?"

"I said *perhaps* from the very start. And I still say it. We don't know what the Kinde Folke will do. There's no understanding them. They're not like us."

"If that's all the comfort you can give me, you might as well leave me to suffer."

There was a brief silence. Then Granny said, "So be it,

Agnes. Truly, I have done all I can. But I urge you to go on caring for the changeling. You never know what might happen. There's still hope."

"I am weary of waiting and hoping. Just go and leave me be."

"Good day to you, then." The door closed, and Mam began to sob.

I stayed where I was, thinking she might not want me to see her crying. Afternoon sunlight slanted through the loft's small window, bringing with it the smell of hay, the sound of birdsong, and the heat of summer.

I watched bits of dust dance in the shaft of light and thought about Mam's longing to have Thomas back. What if, what if—what if I took Guest away and went in search of Thomas? Suppose I found the Kinde Folke and persuaded them to take Guest and give me Thomas? Surely they'd see Mam had treated Guest well. Wasn't it possible they had some kindness in their hearts?

But how was I to find the Kinde Ones? They might be across the sea and far away. Then again, they might be just over the next hill. Those ones traveled here and there in the Dark Lands, sometimes staying in one place, sometimes in another. The villagers said the Kinde Folke did not want to be found. But had anyone ever been brave enough to seek them?

Perhaps in old tales there were those who did, but not in our ordinary life. Certainly not girls like me.

Truth to tell, it scared me to think of going off on my own. I'd never been farther from home than Lower Hexham, just a mile down the road. On the other side of the village was Mirkwood, where even the bravest boys dared not go. And beyond Mirkwood were the Dark Lands.

If it hadn't been for me, my brother would be in Mam's arms, and Dadoe would be smoking his pipe in the garden. And the changeling would be — well, wherever he should be, not here.

So, no matter how scared I was, I had to make things right. Me, Mollie Cloverall, all by myself, I would rescue my baby brother.

I found Mam downstairs, nursing Guest. Too sad and weary to turn her head, she didn't notice me, but the changeling gazed at me with his yellow eyes, as watchful as a cat.

"Soon you'll be gone," I mouthed at him. "You hateful thing."

He closed his eyes and gave all of his attention to Mam and the milk he sucked from her.

"I'll fix supper, Mam," I said. "Is there anything you'd like to eat?"

Still without really seeing me, she shook her head. "I haven't got much appetite."

After she'd eaten a bit of bread and half a bowl of soup, she lay down on her bed. For once, Guest was sleeping, and I was glad to see Mam using the time to rest.

After supper, I pumped a pail of water from the well and washed the dishes. When the kitchen was clean and tidy, I went outside and stood by the gate. Across the fields, Mirkwood lay deep in shadow. Birds chirped in the hedgerows, and tall stalks of purple foxglove swayed gently, still humming with the last of the day's bees. The moon had already risen, pale-faced in the sky, almost full. The smell of wet grass sweetened the air.

In the distance, farm workers trudged home, their voices and laughter barely audible. Dadoe should have been with them, but he was far away, working in unknown fields with strangers.

Gripping the gate with both hands, I wished on the first

star of the night. *Please let me find the Kinde Folke, please let them take Guest and return Thomas, please let me bring him safely home, please let Dadoe return and Mam laugh and be happy. Please, oh please, a thousand times please, let everything be the same as it was.*

4

THE NEXT MORNING, MAM carried Guest outside and laid him on Thomas's quilt. For once, he lay still and watched the clouds float by in the shape of endless flocks of fluffy sheep.

Crouching behind a bush, I spied on Guest while I weeded the garden. I was sure he didn't know I was nearby. Perhaps if I waited long enough, Guest might, just might, reveal something. Surely he had secrets. Maybe he knew where the Kinde Folke were. Maybe they talked to him and he to them.

A fly landed on my nose, and I brushed it away before it made me sneeze. Ants paraded across my foot, tickling my toes. Beads of sweat trickled down my back. The sun was hot and the air heavy with summer. Bees buzzed in the foxgloves as if they were trying to lull me to sleep.

Guest began wailing softly, not a cry, not a shriek, but a sad sound that rose and fell, not quite sobs, not quite a tune.

The song drifted across the garden and over the wall. It mingled with the breeze and the rustle of leaves; it ran with the stream over rocks; it mingled with the singing of birds and the humming of bees.

Sorrowful it was and beautiful. I'd never heard anything quite like it, certainly not from Guest.

The song ended as suddenly as it began. Guest turned his head toward my hiding place. His yellow eyes found me and held me fast. Silent now and sly, he looked at me as if daring me to come closer.

I got to my feet and stared down at him. "Where did you learn that song?"

He kept his gaze on me. His expression didn't change. Nor did he answer. Not that I'd expected him to.

"I might as well ask the cat." I leaned over him, my face mere inches from his. "I don't know what you see when you look at me like that. Do you know what *I* see when I look at *you*?"

His face became secretive.

"I see an ugly, ill-natured creature." I spat out the words as if they were poison. "An imp from the devil, as ugly as Thomas was beautiful, as nasty as Thomas was sweet."

A magpie in the hedgerow cocked its head at me. Its wings stirred, as if the bird was ready to fly away to the Kinde Folke.

No, I must not speak harshly to Guest or harm him in any way—not while Thomas was a prisoner of the Kinde Folke.

Mam came to the door and looked out. "Is everything all right?" she asked—meaning, *Was Guest safe?*

"Everything is fine," I lied.

At the sound of Mam's voice, Guest began to shriek. He kicked and waved his fists.

Bending over him, Mam picked him up with difficulty, as if he'd grown too heavy for her. "Surely you're not hungry again?"

His answer was to strike her with his flailing fists and tear open her dress.

By that evening, Mam scarcely had the energy to eat her supper. Her eyes were nearly as sunken as Granny Hedgepath's, and blue shadows discolored the skin under them. Her hair, once thick and shiny, hung limp in uncombed strings around her pale face. Her dress hung on her thin body.

• • •

Late that night, I wrote Mam a letter:

> I have taken Guest and gone to find Thomas. Do not worry—I will be safe and I will bring Thomas home and leave Guest with them that he belongs to.
> Please eat and rest whilst I am gone and get strong.
> Love from your daughter, Mollie

Quietly I filled a canvas bag with a loaf of bread, a jug of milk and one of water, a hunk of yellow cheese, and six apples. I didn't dare take more, for we didn't have much.

I touched the locket hidden under my dress. Perhaps I could use it to barter with the Kinde Folke. Like magpies and crows, they probably liked shiny things.

I tiptoed to the cradle. Guest lay still, but his eyes were open, shining like a cat's in the dark.

Expecting a struggle that would wake Mam, I wrapped him tight in a blanket that I slung onto my back. Without so much as a whimper, he let me carry him from the cottage.

The dirt road was white in the moonlight, and the

foxgloves that bordered it were black. Everything else dissolved in shades of gray—the fields quilting the hillsides, the stone walls, the grass. The only sound was the cry of an owl somewhere up ahead.

At the top of Cat Tail Hill, I turned and looked back at our cottage, so small at the foot of the hill. I'd never spent a night away from Mam. Now here I was about to set out on a journey with no clear idea of where I was going. Or when I'd be back. Or *if* I'd be back.

But on I trudged, downhill and into the village. The moon silvered its thatched roofs. Windows were dark. Not a single candle shone. I felt like a burglar creeping from cottage to cottage, choosing which one to enter and rob.

A dog barked on a narrow side street. A cat peered down at me from a high stone wall, eyes agleam. In one house, someone snored loudly enough for me to hear.

I paused to shift Guest to a better position. He'd still not made a sound, but he tightened his grip and dug his fingernails into my shoulders. This close, I smelled his wildness and quickened my steps. The sooner I found the Kinde Folke, the sooner I'd be rid of the creature on my back.

As we neared the old stone bridge that spanned the river,

I saw a horse and cart stopped in the middle. The peddler leaned against the wall and played a pennywhistle. On my back, Guest shifted his position to look over my shoulder.

When the peddler saw me, he smiled, but instead of greeting me, he continued to play a melancholy tune. The music seemed familiar, but I didn't know where I'd heard it, only that I had. Guest dug his feet into my back and reared up to get a better look at the peddler.

Lowering the whistle, the peddler said, "Well, well, if it's not little Mollie Cloverall with the travelers' babby on her back. What brings you out so late at night? Not to buy ribbons and beads and flowers, I wager."

"The creature won't sleep unless I walk him about in the moonlight." I was surprised at how quickly the lie fell from my mouth. "It soothes him."

"Ah, I've known a few babbies like that." He reached over my shoulder to pat Guest's head.

"Careful," I warned him. "Sometimes he bites."

The old man laughed. "No fear. The meanest dog in the world knows better than to bite me."

I took a step to pass the peddler, but he stopped me. "If I were you, I wouldn't go any farther. The crossroads lie just ahead and beyond them is Mirkwood, both dangerous places for a lass and a babby on a dark night like this."

"Oh, I won't go farther than the bend in the road." I pointed ahead to a place where the road curved.

"You wouldn't be fibbing to me, would you?"

I crossed my fingers behind my back and shook my head. "No, sir, that I would not."

"Take care as you go, then." He stepped out of my way and doffed his yellow hat. Its black feather bobbed. "May no harm come to either of you."

With relief, I crossed the bridge and glanced back to see if the peddler watched me, but he'd already turned toward the village. His horse's hooves rang on the stone, and its harness bells jingled.

All too soon, the road curved and the village was behind me, no more than a huddle of cottages by the side of the road, now as small as heaps of stones left by children. Ahead, just over the hill was Mirkwood. Hitching Guest higher on my back, I climbed the road to the top. From there I looked down on the dark forest. It stretched as far as I could see, bordered by the sea on the far side and the Dark Lands on the other.

Again Guest hoisted himself high enough to see over my head. He yelped like a fox or a wolf, a strange incomprehensible sound. From the forest, an owl hooted as if in answer.

Going downhill, I picked up speed until, stumbling on loose stones, I forced myself to go slower. It wouldn't do to fall.

At the bottom of the hill were the crossroads, dark with sorrow and foreboding.

Those who'd killed themselves were buried in this place. Murderers, too, and thieves, all those who weren't allowed to lie in churchyards. Changelings and unwanted babies both had been left here to die. If any place was haunted, the crossroads was.

Moaning softly, Guest clung to me and rocked back and forth as if he feared I meant to leave him here.

I wished I could do exactly that, but I was almost certain the Kinde Folke would take him and give me Thomas.

As soon as we left the crossroads behind, Guest loosened his grip and stopped moaning and rocking. Very still now, he crouched behind me as a frightened animal might.

For the first time, I felt a twinge of pity, a very small one, for certainly Guest had caused a great deal of hardship in our family and did not deserve my sympathy.

Catching light from the moon, white stones lined the path into the forest. After a few steps, darkness closed around me. I kept my eyes on the stones, afraid of what I might see if I looked between the trees on either side of me.

Guest resumed moaning. He seemed to be as frightened as I was.

Things moved in the shadows, too far from the path for me to see what they were. I hoped they stayed where they were.

On my back, Guest moved restlessly and muttered to himself. His warm breath tickled my neck. With every step I took, he seemed heavier and my legs felt weaker. I longed to be rid of him.

Too weary to go on, I eased Guest from my back and sank down to rest against the smooth side of a mossy rock.

Guest huddled beside me, clicking and clacking to himself. Sometimes he glanced at me as if he expected me to understand him, but the noises didn't sound like words to me.

"If only you could tell me where to find the Kinde Folke," I said. "But you can't talk. And you can't walk. What use are you to me or anyone?"

Guest hung his head and stared silently at the ground.

For a moment, he reminded me of a lamb I'd once raised because its mother refused to nurse it. *A useless runt*, Dadoe called it. He told me to let it die, but I nursed it with a rag soaked in milk. When it was too big for me to carry, I let it go back to the flock.

But Guest was not a lamb. He was a wicked creature, unwanted by his mother or anyone else. He didn't deserve my pity.

I squatted beside him and looked into his eyes. "Do you know where we're going?"

Guest peered at me, wild and strange.

"I'm taking you back to your own people, the ones who didn't want you, the ones who took my brother and left you in his place. The 'Kinde Folke' they're called, though they are not kind at all. I'll trade you for my brother and be rid of you forever."

Guest made a mournful sound and curled into a small ball. Had he understood what I'd said? No, I told myself, he had no more intelligence than a dumb animal.

I poked him as if he were a sleeping dog. "Can I trust you to stay with me if I sleep?"

Guest curled up even smaller and covered his big ears with his hands.

I poked him again, harder this time. "You had better be here when I wake up."

No answer, not even a look. If I'd had a rope, I'd have tied him to a tree.

I covered him with the blanket I'd used for a sling and pulled another for myself from my canvas bag.

I'd sleep for a while and then go on. Soon we'd find the Kinde Folke. I was sure of it. Well, almost sure.

When I opened my eyes, morning had come and Guest was gone. I leapt to my feet and gazed into the misty forest. The trees had kept their vigil. They still stood tall and straight, but where was the changeling?

"Guest," I called. "Guest—where are you?" My voice bounced from one tree trunk to the next, but I heard no answer. I called again and again, peering into the mist but afraid to leave the path.

A few days ago, I'd have been happy Guest was gone, but without him I had nothing to trade for Thomas. I might as well go home. I opened my bag and pulled out the water jug. Before I'd taken my first sip, I saw Guest. He'd burrowed into the ferns like a fawn and almost buried himself in a hollow under a boulder. His back was to me, and he seemed sound asleep.

Angry at the trick he'd played, I shouted, "Wake up!"

He turned and looked at me, blank-faced as usual, and crawled slowly from his hiding place. The first thing he did was grab the milk jug from the bag.

I yanked the jug away from him, removed the top, and held him while he drank. Such a greedy creature he was. Guzzle, guzzle, guzzle.

"You can't drink it all," I told him. "I doubt we'll find a cow in Mirkwood."

He shrieked and screamed and flailed about just as he did at home, biting, pinching, and kicking. It took all my strength to swaddle him in the blanket and hoist him onto my back.

As I walked, I ate a small piece of cheese while Guest screamed.

Ahead of us, the ground rose steeply. Warm damp air clung to me, and midges too tiny to see bit my face, my ears, my neck.

Guest continued to wail and snort and snuffle. He squirmed and twisted, throwing his weight from one side to the other. I didn't dare turn and look at him for fear I'd throw him into the ravine that bordered the path.

On we went, mile after weary mile. The farther I walked, the more the trees closed in around us. Very little daylight found its way through their leafy tops. Guest and I seemed to move through endless twilight, with no idea of the time —morning, noon, evening—but not night, not yet.

Sometimes I walked between boulders that towered over us, their surfaces softened by thick coats of moss. Trees grew from the tops of some. Their roots twisted down the sides, digging into crevices. Water dripped from the rocks and pooled on the path. I wished I'd thought to bring a walking stick to keep my balance.

At the top of yet another hill, I felt Guest's body tense. His grip on my shoulders tightened. Very softly he began to make a series of clacking sounds.

At the bottom of the hill, a man leaned against a boulder, watching us make our way toward him. While he waited, he played a mournful tune on a tin whistle. The music put me in mind of the song Guest had sung in the garden.

From what I could see of the man, half-hidden as he was in the tall ferns, he seemed a harmless sort, a wandering musician perhaps. I'd seen his like playing tunes on market day, a cap beside him to catch coins tossed by generous folk.

Keeping my eyes on my feet, I made my way slowly and carefully down the treacherous path. It was my hope that the man might know the whereabouts of the Kinde Folke. Perhaps he would lead me to them. A bit of company would be a pleasure, especially if he was willing to carry Guest for at least part of the way.

5

Up close, the man was neither handsome nor ugly, neither old nor young, but somewhere in between. He wore a faded black hat with a wide brim. The sleeves of his green jacket were frayed, the fabric faded. The knees of his pants were patched and his boots well-worn. A shapeless pack lay beside him.

I came nearer. But not too near. He had the sly eyes of a clever fox, I thought, and I wasn't sure I could trust him after all.

Guest pushed himself up to see over my shoulder. He burst into a series of loud clicks and clacks.

"He can't talk," I said, but the stranger paid me no mind.

Instead he imitated Guest, as if he were mocking him.

Guest's eyes glowed as if someone had lit a lamp in his brain. He waved his thin arms and bounced up and down in his sling until I feared he'd knock me over. Crowing and chirping, the two of them chittered and chattered until the trees around us echoed the din. My head ached with the sound.

Finally, the man raised his hand and turned his palm toward Guest. Immediately Guest fell silent, but his gaze was fixed on the man.

"Were you *talking* to him?" I asked.

"Ah, I was just fooling with him the way you might meow at a cat." The man shifted his sly eyes back to Guest. "He's an odd babby if ever I saw one. And no kin to you, I'm sure. What do you call him?"

"Guest is his name."

"Guest? A strange name for a strange babby."

"It's what he is. A guest in our home."

"And where are you taking him so far from any house?"

"I hope to find his people. Travelers they are. He's outstayed his welcome at our house." This stranger asked too many questions, and I was giving him answers as fast as he asked for them. He had a way of drawing words from my mouth like a conjurer doing tricks with scarves and coins.

"I see, I see." The man rocked back and forth on his heels

as if he were thinking this over. "The travelers left him with you. Is that the way of it?"

Hitching Guest higher on my back, I said, "Yes, that's indeed the way of it, and though it's been a pleasure to know you this little bit, we must be going on now."

"You're seeking the . . ." He paused a moment and grinned once more like a clever fox. "The *travelers*, I believe you said?"

"Aye, the travelers." I moved to the side to step around the man, but he stepped the same way and blocked me. Feeling frightened now, I said, "Please, sir, let us go by."

Without moving, he said, "Perhaps I can help a wee lass, deep in Mirkwood, far from home, and toting a big babby that weighs as much as she does."

"I've done well enough so far without your help."

"But do you have even an inkling of where these so-called *travelers* might be?"

"Somewhere ahead. Not far, I'm sure." I stood my ground but shivered with cold. The heavy air of night had begun to sink into the forest like a dark fog, filling the spaces between the trees and making it hard to see. I was so tired of walking, so tired of carrying Guest. And hungry. My belly craved to be filled with cheese and bread.

"It seems you're too weary to take another step," the man said. "Sit you here by this rock, and I'll make a fire to drive off the evening chill. There's a pair of skinned hares in my sack, ready to cook for supper. Will you join me?"

My head told me not to say yes to the stranger's offer, but my belly shouted, *Yes, sit down, let him build a fire, let him cook the hares. Eat. Get warm. Rest.*

And so, I slid the sling off my weary shoulders. Guest crouched beside his new friend and peered into his face as if to memorize every feature.

I sank down on the ground and leaned against the mossy rock, which was not as soft as it looked, and also a bit cold and damp. But it felt good to watch the stranger lay a fire.

When the flames leapt up, sending a fountain of sparks into the dark leaves overhead, the man turned to me. "You've never told me your name," he said.

"Nor have you told me yours."

He smiled and spitted the hares. As they began to cook, the smell of roasting meat made my stomach rumble.

"Will you or won't you tell me your name?" he asked.

"Only if you tell me yours." I knew better than to tell a

stranger my name unless he told me his. Knowing a name gives you power over its owner.

The man leapt to his feet and bowed. "I'm called Madog Ashe, Esquire, a wanderer by choice with no place to call my own, as at home in a forest as in a village. Perhaps more so."

I didn't get up, and even if I had, I wouldn't have returned his bow with a curtsy. "I'm Mollie Cloverall from the village of Lower Hexham, just over the way from Upper Hexham."

"And your people? Who are they?"

"My father is Sam Cloverall, a farmer, and my mother is Agnes."

"And why have they sent a wee lass such as you to return the travelers' babby?"

I shrugged. "Someone had to take him."

"And what do you aim to get from the travelers in return for their babby?" Madog asked.

"My— I mean, nothing. Nothing at all. I just want Guest to be gone forever from our home."

"Why is it I feel you're hiding something from me?"

I picked up a stick and poked at the fire. Guest squatted beside me and began pinching my arms. I swatted his hands away, and he nipped my cheek with his little teeth.

Madog made a sharp noise and clapped his hands. Immediately Guest reached out to him and began his babble of strange sounds. "Come now, Mollie. This is no travelers' babby," Madog said. "Why lie about it? He's a changeling left with your family by the Kinde Folke. Did you think I wouldn't know his true nature?"

I took the roasted leg of hare Madog offered and began to gnaw the meat from it, tough and stringy as it was. "I said what I said, for some people have a strong dislike of changelings."

"You don't seem to like him much yourself."

"I despise him—he's hateful and nasty, and he drove Dadoe from our house and wore my mother down to almost nothing. But you see, it's my fault the Kinde Folke took my brother. I plan to set things right again."

"And how do you aim to do that?"

"If you must know, I mean to swap the changeling for my brother."

Madog shook his head. "I'm a man who knows much more about the Kinde Folke than you do." He leaned across the fire to see me better. His eyes reflected the flames.

I turned my head to the side so as not to look into their green depths. A person could drown in eyes like Madog's.

Madog stirred the fire so the flames leapt up again and lit his face from below. "The Kinde Folke will most certainly not trade your brother for the changeling. You'd best turn around tomorrow and go home."

"I cannot go home without Thomas." I reached into my dress and showed him the locket on its silver chain. "I'll trade this as well as Guest for him."

Madog startled me by jumping back from the locket. "Put that away," he said. "The Kinde Folke won't give you anything for that. They cannot bear the touch of iron. Nor can I or Guest. Keep it tucked away so as not to harm us."

"But it's not iron, it's silver."

"It's silver on the outside but iron underneath. Show it to Guest. Don't touch him with it. Just hold it in front of him."

The moment Guest saw the locket, he covered his face with his hands and began to howl as if I'd hurt him.

I slipped the locket back inside my dress and looked at Madog.

"Iron is poison to Kinde Folke and anyone who shares their blood. That includes travelers and changelings. Keep it close to you always—it will protect you from them and their creatures."

Once the locket was out of sight, Guest began pinching and biting me again. His teeth had grown sharp, and it was all I could do not to slap him. Thrusting the jug of milk into his mouth, I muttered, "Go on, little pig, but, mind you, there'll be no more when it's gone."

"Guest has teeth," Madog said. "He should be weaned." Pulling a piece of tender meat from the rabbit's carcass, he held it in front of Guest. "Try this."

The changeling looked at the tasty morsel dangling in front of his nose. Casting aside the jug, he grabbed the meat and sniffed. Into his mouth it went.

"You see?" Madog asked me. "Guest won't starve. He'll eat what you eat, right enough."

I watched Guest chew the meat and swallow it down. All that remained in my bag was a bit of cheese and a stale crust of bread, not enough for me, let alone to share with him.

Madog winked at Guest and began to speak again in sharp bits and bites of harsh sounds.

Guest cocked his head as if he understood. Turning his yellow eyes to me, he said, "Mollie." He touched Madog's face. "Madog." Pointing to himself, he said, "Guest."

His voice was high and raspy, and he spoke fast, but I understood him.

"He speaks better in his own language," Madog said, "but he'll learn yours fast enough. He already understands more than you realize."

Turning back to Guest, Madog lifted him to his feet. "Show Mollie what else you can do."

For a moment the changeling stood there, wobbling a bit, getting his balance like an overgrown toddler. Finally, drawing a deep breath, he took one step and then another. After he'd tottered all the way around the fire, he collapsed next to Madog, in a heap of scrawny legs and arms, and gave me a sly grin.

"You little beast." I was so angry, I almost slapped him. "To think I carried you all this way!"

Madog laughed. "For sure, the rascal has more tricks than I do. And that's saying something!"

"It's not funny. My back hurts from carrying him. He's heavy, and he wiggles and squirms and kicks and pinches. He made me stumble and almost fall over and over again."

"Now, Mollie. Don't be angry with him. How could he

keep up with you? Surely a fox would catch him and gobble him up."

I looked at Guest, annoyed that he'd tricked me. "He's big enough now to keep up with me. And what fox would eat a bundle of skin and bones like him?"

"Enough of this complaining," Madog said. "You've both come a long, hard way today, and this little scamp must be tired out." He raised his hand, palm facing Guest. "Lie down and sleep."

Without a word, Guest lay down on his blanket. His eyes closed, he breathed deeply and evenly, and he slept.

"I wish Mam had known that trick. She might have gotten more sleep."

"True enough." Madog leaned back on one elbow and stared at me across the fire. "From what he tells me, I understand Guest has not heard one kind word from you or your mam. She fed him, and you watched over him, but neither of you had any thought except getting Thomas back. You, Mollie, would have killed him if you'd dared. Don't deny it."

"We wanted our Thomas," I said in a low, shamed voice, "not Guest. Wouldn't anyone? At least we didn't leave him at the crossroads as some do."

"True enough, but a wee bit of kindness—was that too much to give him?"

"You weren't there, you didn't hear him scream and cry without end. He was at Mam, all day and all night, sucking like a greedy pig. No matter how much milk she gave him, it was never enough. He was killing her."

Madog sighed. "The poor pitiful creature wasn't made for human milk. Hungry he was, but the more he ate, the more his belly ached. Is it any wonder he screamed day and night?"

"Why isn't he screaming now, then?"

"He's drinking cow's milk from that jug you brought. That's all you had to do, you know. Give him cow's milk."

"Too bad you weren't around to tell us."

Madog sighed. "I didn't know you had him, did I?"

"Well, I won't have him for long. I'll find the Kinde Folke soon, and they'll take him. They will! And I'll go home with Thomas."

He shook his head, and his shadow moved against the rock behind him. "The ones you seek are far from here and hard to find. They don't look kindly on mortals who cross the border into their land."

"Isn't Mirkwood their land? Isn't it where they live?"

"Mortals and Kinde Folke alike come and go in Mirkwood. The Kinde Folke's land lies on the other side."

"If you know so much, why can't you take Guest and me to them?"

"The Kinde Folke bear a grudge against me. It would do more harm than good for me to lead you there. But I can tell you how to find them."

The firelight played with his face, lighting his nose, then an eye, then his chin, making him waver as if he were a shadow himself or a ripple on water.

"Who are you, anyway? Who are your people? Where do you come from?"

"Let's say I'm a man you don't meet every day."

"And glad I am of that. Meeting one of you every day would indeed be misery."

"You're not the first to say that, and I'm sure you won't be the last."

Stirring the fire, Madog created a fountain of sparks between us.

"Do you have dealings with the Kinde Folke?" I asked in a low voice.

"Perhaps." Madog drew his tin whistle from his pocket and began to play his mournful tune.

Too tired to ask more questions, I stopped struggling to keep my eyes open. With a sigh, I lay down in the moss and ferns and fell at once into a deep sleep. If I had dreams, I did not remember them.

6

I WOKE TO A GRAY mist that hid everything more than a few feet beyond the end of my nose. The fire had gone out, and my clothes were wet and cold, and so was I. All around me, water dripped and dropped from trees. *Plink, plunk, plink.* The smell of mold and damp earth and moss hung in the air.

Guest huddled by the fire's ashes, as cold and wet as I was, snuffling in his sleep like a sick calf.

"Madog?" I called. "Madog, where are you?"

My voice rang in the mist, but Madog didn't answer.

Guest sat up and looked at me. "Madog gone."

"Gone? Gone where?"

"Gone," he said. "Gone. Madog gone."

"Maybe he's just hunting rabbits for breakfast?"

"No! Madog gone. Gone, gone, gone!" Guest's voice rose to a shriek.

I seized his narrow shoulders and peered into his yellow

eyes, searching for a different answer. "What will we do without Madog to help us? How will we eat, how will we know which way to go?"

Guest pointed to my sack. "Food."

I sighed in frustration but kept my temper. "We ate everything last night."

"Food!" Guest pushed himself up on his spindly bowlegs and toddled toward the sack. He tried to lift it, but it was too heavy.

I ran to help him. Bread, cheese, jugs of milk and water, apples, walnuts, and dried meat tumbled out of the sack.

"Did Madog leave this for us?"

"For me." He paused and gave me a squint-eyed grin. "And you."

I doled out portions for us and tied the rest up in the sack. "We have to make this last," I told Guest. "If we gobble it all up now, we'll be very hungry when it's gone."

Guest patted his belly. "Hungry now."

"What did I just tell you? We have to make it last!"

"Madog bring more," Guest said.

"Did he tell you that?"

He shrugged. "No. Yes."

I fought an urge to shake an answer out of him. "Which is it—yes or no?"

Guest shrugged again.

"Maybe, is that what you mean?"

"Maybe maybe maybe."

I tried another question. "Did Madog tell you which way we should go to find your people?"

Guest pointed to the path.

With a sigh, I prepared to hoist Guest onto my back, but he pulled away from me.

"I walk."

I knew he'd not walk far. Not on those bandy little legs. But the more he walked, the less I had to carry him.

Without Guest on my back, I put my sack into the sling, and we set off into the fog. Warm moist air clung to me. Clouds of midges circled our heads. Whenever we stopped to rest, the midges doubled and tripled in number and forced us to keep moving.

Guest began to slow down and lag behind. When he tottered and almost fell, I hoisted him into the sling along with the sack of food. With his weight on my back and his smell in my nose, I breathed the changeling in with every step I took.

For fear of stumbling, I didn't dare to raise my eyes above the ground under my feet. Sometime after noon, I found myself high above a mist-filled valley. Willing my legs not to tremble, I steadied myself against a rock wall and tried to breathe normally.

Just ahead, a waterfall poured in separate streams over a tall, dark rockface. It seemed to fall from the sky itself and crash to earth far below.

The noise of the water woke Guest, and he moved about in the sling.

"Be still," I cried. "You'll make me trip, and we'll go over the edge."

"Not trip, no." For once, Guest did what I asked and stayed as still as our sack of food.

Slowly I made my way downhill. I did not look at the edge of the cliff. I did not look at the waterfall. I looked at nothing but my feet and the rocks and roots on the path.

At the bottom of the hill, I loosened the sling, and Guest slid to the ground.

The fog turned to a cold, hard rain.

Guest began to whimper. "Cold. Wet. Hungry."

Off to the left was a large dark lake. At one end, the waterfall turned its surface to foam. To the right, rocks thrust up through tall grass like giant fingers reaching for the sky.

"We'll shelter here," I said.

As I spoke, thunder boomed and lightning dove from the clouds, splitting into dozens of forks. At the same moment, the wind rose and drove icy needles of rain into our faces.

With Guest behind me, I plunged into the tall grass and made my way toward three tall rocks huddled together like old men. Squeezing through a narrow opening between two of them, we tumbled into a small sheltered place. Grass had grown on top of the rocks, forming a roof of sorts, and the earth was mossy and dry.

In the dim light, I saw piles of leaves and dry branches that must have blown in long ago. Gathering some of them, I took out the flint Madog had left in the sack of food. I'd had some experience lighting a fire, but it took a long time to coax the flames big enough to warm us.

I laid our blanket out to dry and took food from the sack. Carrots, apples, cheese, and dried meat made a decent meal for the two of us.

By the time we'd eaten, our clothes were almost dry. Guest

dozed where he sat, his head nodding on his spindly neck like a flower too heavy for its stalk.

He was a sad sight, but I had no pity for him. It was his fault we were here, cold and miserable, his fault I was lying on hard ground with rain dripping in my face, his fault Thomas was gone.

With my mind full of wicked thoughts, I glared at Guest's back. There he lay, the cause of everything wrong in my life, sleeping peacefully while I lay awake. I could barely wait to be rid of him.

Pulling my blanket over me, I listened to the rain pound the rocks. Wind howled in every crack and did its best to blow out the fire. Thunder crashed and banged and boomed.

Beneath the racket of the storm, I became aware of a faint sound. I sat up and listened closely. Somewhere a horse whinnied. As it came closer, I heard its hooves strike the earth.

Guest stirred in his sleep and sat up, half-awake but clearly frightened. "What that noise?"

"A horse," I told him. "What's it doing here in the middle of the night?"

Guest turned his head from side to side, listening hard.

He sniffed and tensed like a hunting dog who's caught the scent of something.

"Not horse."

"Of course it's a horse. Hear it whinny? Hear its hooves?"

Guest dove under his blanket. "Hide, hide. Something's wrong."

"What do you mean?" He was beginning to scare me.

"Hide, Mollie. A bad thing out there."

Now I was scared too, but just as I pulled my blanket over my head, I heard Madog calling my name.

I tossed off the blanket and jumped up. "It's Madog! He's back!"

In a muffled voice, Guest said, "No. Not Madog."

"It *is* Madog. You must be even stupider than I thought."

Madog called again. "Come to me, Mollie."

Guest reached out from under the blanket and grabbed my skirt. "Not Madog! Stay here."

"Let go of me, you mooncalf." I pulled away and ran to the opening in the rocks.

Madog's voice sang in my ears. *Mollie, Mollie, Mollie, come to me, Mollie.* The words twisted around me like a spell and drew me outside.

And there was Madog, sitting high on the back of the biggest and most beautiful black horse I'd ever seen. His head seemed to touch the sky; his mane hid the hills.

Leaving Guest wailing, I ran to Madog as lightly as if I were flying. The horse bowed down to me. His breath was warm and sweet with the fragrance of fresh-cut grass.

"Climb up," Madog said, "climb up and travel with me to my kingdom across the silver sea."

I sat on the horse's broad back, and he rose to his feet and began to gallop away from the stones where I'd left Guest.

I turned to smile at Madog, but he wasn't sitting behind me as I'd thought. "Madog," I cried. "Where are you?"

The only answer was a faint cry from Guest.

"Whoa," I shouted to the horse. "Where is Madog?"

But the horse paid me no heed. He galloped with such speed, the world blurred and I couldn't see the rocks or the lake.

"Put me down!" I screamed. "Stop!"

The horse ran faster and faster yet. It was as if we'd left the ground and were riding up into the sky. The horse ripped the rain apart like a curtain and climbed cloud mountains.

Leaping streams of stars, he flew higher and higher until I thought we'd land on the moon.

Terrified of falling, I clung to his mane. "Where are you taking me?"

His whinny sounded like a laugh. "You chose to answer my call, Mollie. You chose to ride with me. You are mine now."

"What sort of a horse talks? What are you truly?"

"You should know what I am."

"Take me back to earth," I cried. "Please. I beg you! I'm afraid."

Onward we went. In and out of clouds, our path lit with lightning, my ears deaf from thunder. I held his mane so tightly, my fingers ached.

"Please," I sobbed, "please."

"Are you certain you wish me to take you back?"

"Yes, yes."

"You will have your wish, Mollie." Down from the stars he flew. Beneath me, I saw the lake's black water, its surface laced with silver ripples. At first sight, the lake was no bigger than a rain puddle, but as we plunged toward it, it grew larger. I understood that the horse meant to dive into the lake and drown me.

I lunged to one side, but the black threads of his mane wrapped themselves around me and held me fast. Into the water we plunged, going so deep, I thought I'd never see the sky again.

As I struggled to escape, I felt the locket press against my skin. I didn't know if such a small thing would work against a mighty stallion, but I felt dizzy, lightheaded, as if I were half-dead already. Pulling it from my dress, I used all my strength to push the silver heart against the horse's neck.

With a shudder, the stallion threw me from his back. Freeing myself from his mane, I struggled to escape his thrashing hooves. The water was dark and murky. Reeds and grasses wrapped themselves around my legs. I wasn't sure what direction I was going—up to the surface or down to the bottom.

With the last of my strength, I burst out of the water. Rain struck my face. I coughed and choked. The lake rose and fell in waves, but I saw the shore only a few feet away.

All I knew about swimming was to kick my feet and paddle with my hands, but I managed to crawl out of the water. I lay still for a moment, gulping mouthfuls of air. I didn't dare stay where I was for fear the stallion might come after me.

I staggered away from the lake, but I didn't get very far

before the stallion splashed out of the water behind me. I didn't know which way to go, so I ran straight ahead, faster than I'd ever run before.

The stallion whinnied, and his hooves pounded the ground. He was gaining on me, close enough for me to smell the lake water clinging to him.

I saw the rock shelter ahead, but I knew the stallion would catch me long before I reached it. Changing direction, I headed toward a grove of small wind-twisted trees, thinking to hide in their tangled branches. Behind me, the stallion snorted. He was so close now, I felt his breath on my neck.

Just as I neared the grove, Madog stepped out from behind a tree and faced the stallion.

Speechless with fear, I hid behind Madog. He was all that stood between me and the horse.

In rage, the stallion reared up on his hind legs and threatened Madog with his hooves.

"Step aside," he cried. "The girl is mine."

I cowered behind Madog and stared into the horse's face. Mighty he was and beautiful and fearsome enough to take my breath away. What chance did either Madog or I have against something so powerful?

Instead of surrendering, Madog held out his hand, his

palm facing the horse. "What do you want with this girl, my friend?"

The horse tossed his head and whinnied. His mane flew about him like a ragged black cloud.

And then, though I scarce believed what I saw, the horse changed to a man as beautiful and wild as the horse. Power seemed to light him from within.

"Madog, I have had dealings with you." His voice was like the storm, thunderous and deep, and I drew closer to Madog, more afraid of the man—if he was a man—than I'd been of the horse.

Madog bent his knee. "Yes, we traded horses long ago when I was a green lad. No sooner had you left with two of my best stallions than the mare you gave me turned into a spindle-legged pony, worth nothing."

The man laughed. "Ah yes. Those horses were a fine bargain, I must say."

Madog did not laugh. "Let's save our reminiscing for another time. Now I ask, why do you waste your time on this mortal?"

"There are some who do not wish this girl to enter their land. She does not belong there, and she brings contamination with her." The man shrugged. "I was asked to stop her."

"Then, why haven't you?"

Another shrug. "I imagined her to be a worthy foe, but now I see she's a child. A puny thing. Let someone of less stature deal with her. She's no risk to me."

Without another word, the man became a mighty horse once more. Wheeling about, he galloped away.

I watched the stallion vanish into the darkness, unsure of what I'd seen. A horse who took me up to the stars and then down to the bottom of the lake, a horse who changed into a man and back into a horse. How could such a thing be?

In confusion, I turned to Madog and asked, "How did you know to come?"

"I have my ways," he said.

"Were you close by?"

"I was far away, tending to business. I had bargains to make and promises to keep or break."

"Then, how?"

Without answering my question, he said, "But look at you, wet and cold and shaking so hard, you can barely stand. You need the warmth of a fire."

Lifting me onto his back, he began walking toward the rock shelter. "Mind you, I cannot come running to rescue foolish girls every time they do something reckless."

"I'm sorry, Madog, but how could I hide in the rocks when you sat on his back and called to me?"

He shook his head. "Oh, Mollie, surely you've heard tales of the Pookas who live in dark lakes and take lasses like you?"

"Yes, but I'd never seen one, had I? Nor did I think they existed in the real world."

"Well, now you know that Pookas are real, maybe not in Lower Hexham but here in Mirkwood and beyond." He paused a moment as if to give me time to think about what he'd said. "I hope you've also learned what the Kinde Folke will do to stop you from entering their Dark Lands."

I pulled the locket from under my dress. "I saved myself with this. I'll do the same to the Kinde Folke."

"Do not count on the locket too much. You took the Pooka by surprise, that's all. It was I who saved you from being trampled under his hooves. And not a word of thanks have I heard from you."

"Oh, Madog, I do thank you. I promise I'll never be so foolish again."

"You must not trust anyone—man, woman, or child. In this land, things are not always what they seem to be."

7

I MUST HAVE FALLEN ASLEEP, because when I opened my eyes, I was in the stone shelter, covered by blankets, warm and dry and safe. Madog tended the fire, and Guest sat beside him, chattering away in his odd caws and clicks.

When Guest saw my eyes open, he said, "I telled you not to go. You mooncalf, not me."

Madog shook his head at Guest. "I think Mollie knows she should have listened to you. Next time perhaps she will."

Guest thumped his chest. "I knows more than Mollie Mooncalf."

"Oh, be quiet," I muttered. "You were just scared, that's all. You don't know anything."

Guest climbed into Madog's lap. "Mollie Mooncalf," he whispered, giving me his sly smile.

I closed my eyes and gritted my teeth. Guest was the mooncalf, not me, but there he was sitting in Madog's lap, and here I was lying in a corner all by myself. Madog liked Guest better than me, just because he knew more about Pookas than I did. It wasn't fair.

When I woke up in the morning, I was still cross. If I hadn't been so hungry, I would have gone in search of the Kinde Folke all by myself.

Guest watched me from the other side of the fire, but I ignored him. The Kinde Folke would never swap him for Thomas. How foolish of me to think they'd want a puny creature like him.

Madog had gone out foraging and found a dozen duck eggs. Along with cheese and bread, they made a good meal.

When we'd eaten, Madog said, "Now I must go back to Port Riverton and settle a deal with a man and a horse."

"Oh, don't go," I begged him. "What if the Pooka comes back? Or something even worse comes?"

"If you remember what I told you, Mollie, you'll come to no harm." Madog put his hands on my shoulders and looked into my eyes. "Trust no one except Guest. Listen to him. He knows more than you think. And certainly more than you know. He's part Kinde Folke himself."

"But you know much more than he does and you're

stronger and you can tame Pookas. What can a weak creature like Guest do to save me?"

Madog looked at me closely. "Why can't you see Guest as anything but a hindrance?"

"Because that's what he is," I muttered. "He's been a hindrance since the day they left him in our garden. He ruined everything. Everything!"

I bit my lip hard to keep myself from crying. "And now you like him better than me just because he knew about the Pooka."

Madog reached out for Guest and pulled him closer. "If you two are going to find the Kinde Folke and live to tell the story of it, you must get along with each other. Or at least try."

He looked at Guest. "Promise me not to call Mollie names."

Guest looked at me. "Yes, I do what you say. No more Mollie Mooncalf and no more Guest Mooncalf."

Something in Guest's strange eyes told me he still thought I was a mooncalf. He just wouldn't say it out loud.

To me, Madog said, "And you, Mollie. Will you promise to listen to what Guest tells you? He was born in the Dark Lands. Knowledge of its ways runs in his veins."

"I'll listen," I muttered, but I didn't say I'd believe Guest.

Kinde Folke lied—if their blood ran in his veins, how was I to trust their changeling?

Lifting his pack, Madog said, "Pack up your things. We'll start out together, but in a few miles the path splits, and I'll go my way."

We walked silently through the forest. Over our heads the branches of the trees interlaced, blocking most of the light. The only birds I heard were crows quarreling with one another. Every step took us closer to the Dark Lands, and I was more afraid than I cared to admit.

We stopped at a tilted signpost, furred with moss and lichens, pointing west to Port Riverton.

"This is where we part." Madog turned to the west. "I take this way, and you take that."

"But nothing's written on the other side to show me where to go," I said.

"There's only one way to go, and that's straight ahead," Madog told me. "We're at the border of the Dark Lands. One more step and you'll be in their world and at their mercy."

I didn't like the sound of *at their mercy*. "Can you at least tell me how much farther it is?"

"It's impossible to say."

I almost stamped my foot in vexation. "Oh, that's a fine answer!"

"Time and distance change here, Mollie. One day, a certain place might be ten miles away. Another day, it might be a hundred miles away."

"In Lower Hexham, what's ten miles one day is ten miles the next day and the day after and the day after that."

"But you're not in Lower Hexham, are you?"

"No, but I wish I were."

"It's not too late to turn back."

I took a deep breath and looked long and hard at him. "I came here to fetch my brother. I won't go home without him."

"Oh, but you're a stubborn one," Madog said. "Even if you find the Kinde Folke, it's not likely they'll return Thomas."

"You don't know that for certain."

"What does anyone know for certain except the sun will set tonight and come up tomorrow?" He patted my shoulder. "We can make good guesses, though."

"A guess is a guess. Mine is just as good as yours."

Madog shook his head in disagreement and hoisted his pack higher. "I must bid you farewell." He doffed his hat.

"Remember, Guest knows more about this place than you do, Mollie. Listen to him. And don't quarrel."

While we talked, Guest sat on the ground catching beetles and releasing them. Now he looked up at Madog, his eyes asquint.

"I stays on path." He glanced at me and shook his head as if to say he had no control over what *I* might do.

"And so will I," I promised.

"All right, then. Good luck to you both, and be wary of all you meet on your way," Madog told us.

In a panic, I took a step after him. "Will we see you again?"

Madog smiled. "Oh, I'm certain we've not seen the last of each other, Mollie Cloverall." He raised his hand in farewell and walked off toward Port Riverton.

With a loud sigh, I took my first step in the Dark Lands, and Guest followed. Without speaking to each other, we continued on our way.

8

At first, the Dark Lands seemed no different from Mirkwood, but as Guest and I walked farther, a mist like a fallen cloud settled over us. Moisture clung in drops to trees and ferns. Color faded into shades of gray, dull and dreary.

It was as if something dark ran under the surface of this land and leaked into the light. I couldn't see it or taste it or touch it, but I felt it.

The close damp air made me weary. My feet grew so heavy, I could barely lift one and put it in front of the other. Guest lagged behind, whimpering to himself.

Too tired to walk farther, I sat down and rested my back against a boulder.

Guest squatted beside me. Without saying a word, he picked up a stick and drew squiggly shapes in the dirt.

"Do you remember anything about the Dark Lands?" I asked.

Guest didn't answer. He'd found a beetle and was trying to make it climb up his stick. I didn't think he'd even heard me.

I nudged his hand, and he dropped the stick. "Don't scare bug, Mollie."

"I asked you what you remember about this place. Is it always gray and damp? Do fierce animals live here? Will they hurt us?"

Guest watched the beetle crawl over his toes. "Music, I remember music. Sad music. Pretty music. They danced."

"Did they teach you the song you sing?"

Guest wrinkled his forehead in thought. "Mam sing that song."

"*My* mam?"

"*My* mam. Not to me. But I listens." He picked up the beetle and cupped it gently in his hands. "My mam not like me. Scream, hit, hurt me."

Raising his head, he looked at me. "Mollie's mam feed me, but doesn't like me. You doesn't like me." For a moment, he looked sad, but then he smiled at the beetle perched on his thumb. "Bugs like me, Madog like me."

I looked at Guest, really looked at him, something I

hadn't ever done. He was still an ugly little thing, no argument there. His skin was pale, his mouth wide and thin-lipped, his teeth small and crooked as a row of pebbles. Flyaway yellow hair hung in his eyes and straggled down his neck.

But the biggest change was his size. Surely he'd grown faster than a human baby. He was still scrawny and bow-legged, but he was already the size of a five-year-old.

He'd stopped hitting and biting. He ate regular food, he trudged along on his two feet, and he seemed to talk better every day.

I watched him play with the beetle. How gentle he was. A village boy would most likely torment a beetle. He'd pull off its wings and legs. Maybe even step on it and laugh. I'd seen them do it just to make girls scream.

But not Guest.

He looked up at me, as if he sensed I was watching him.

I pointed at the beetle. "Your bug is sitting on your nose now. Doesn't that tickle?"

Guest looked cross-eyed at the beetle. He laughed and moved the little creature to a patch of moss. We watched it crawl into the ferns.

"Bug go home," he said. "We go home?"

"When we find Thomas." I stood up and shouldered my pack.

As dusk darkened into night, we made beds for ourselves in a tree's cradle of roots. Guest gathered wood, and I used my flint to light a fire.

By the time we'd eaten our meal of cheese, bread, and an apple each, it was full night. In the Dark Lands, that meant black in a way night never was in Lower Hexham. The ever-present mist hid the stars and the moon, and the trees wove themselves together, trunk and limb, into a black wall. "Look there." Guest pointed. "Something coming."

"Lights," I whispered. "Dozens of them. What is it?"

Guest pulled me down beside him. "Hide."

"But I want to see!" I stood up. The lights twinkled like fireflies, but as they came closer, they were more like tiny lanterns, dancing back and forth, swinging this way and that, now lighting the ground, now lighting the trees with a strange greenish glow. "Look, Guest. Aren't they beautiful?"

Guest tugged me so hard, I toppled down beside him. "Do what Madog say. Listen, Mollie! They come for you."

Even though I longed to stand up and watch them, I

crouched beside him. The lights looked harmless enough, but I'd promised Madog I'd listen to Guest.

As the lights came closer, I saw the creatures holding the lanterns. They weren't as pretty as I'd expected them to be. Wearing tattered leaves and cobwebs, they were wrinkled like old men and women. The air around them echoed with their cries, a high-pitched whine that buzzed in my head and made it impossible to think.

"Mollie, Mollie," they cried. "Come with us. We have a surprise for you, something you long for, something dear to you, your heart's desire. Come, come!"

Guest grabbed my hand and held tight. "Tricks and lies. No listen. Cover ears."

I tried to pull away, crazy now to follow them, sure they'd lead me to Thomas, but Guest had grown stronger. I could not break his grip on me.

All at once, they surrounded us, hundreds of them, no bigger than wasps. They dazzled our eyes with their lanterns and deafened us with their cries. No longer pretending to be friendly, they pinched, they bit. They pulled our hair as if they meant to yank it out. They tore our clothes as if they wished to strip us to our bare skin.

We swatted them, but they swarmed around us like midges. We could do nothing to drive them away or to protect ourselves.

"Locket!" Guest screamed.

In desperation, I yanked the chain from my dress and thrust it into their midst. At its touch, the creatures shrieked in pain and spiraled upward. In seconds, they'd vanished into the darkness of the trees.

"Tinies. Kinde Folke send them," Guest said. "They leads you into swamps and drowns you."

"I've never seen them before, but Dadoe has. He calls them will-o'-the-wisps or hinky punks."

"Good you listen me this time."

I should have thanked him, but I didn't want him to think too much of himself. He was right this time, but maybe not always.

In the morning, I filled the water jug from a stream, and we trudged deeper into the gloomy forest. A crow watched us from a high branch and then flew away silently. I saw him vanish into the gloom, most likely on his way to tell the Kinde Folke where we were.

Guest plodded beside me, his skinny arms swinging by his side, his head down, his ears red from the Tinies' bites.

"How much farther is it?" I asked.

"Far," he said. "Or not far."

"You sound like Madog."

"Madog knows more than me. Much more than you."

"That's because you're a changeling, and I'm not."

We walked on through the endless dim forest. Tree roots humped and twisted across the path, reaching out like long arms and fingers to trip us. Mist clung to our skin and hair, soaking our clothing and all our belongings. It was a wonder Guest and I weren't covered with moss like the trees and the rocks.

No matter how many miles we traveled, we saw no sign of the Kinde Folke. Sometimes we heard distant laughter, sometimes music, but we couldn't tell where it came from. The wind blew oddly, now this way, now that, and the leaves slithered overhead like snakes.

Exhausted, I leaned on a stout stick I'd found along the way. My boots pinched my toes and blistered my heels. My pack chafed my shoulders and weighed too much for the little it held.

Pulling out the water jug, I drank and handed it to Guest.

"Not too much," I warned. "We haven't crossed a stream for miles."

Guest gulped and passed the jug back to me. His ears twitched like a rabbit's. "Listen. Something's making noise."

Guest hand no sooner warned me than I heard a loud rustling in the ferns. They swayed as if the wind were blowing, and out stepped a person I never expected to see in the Dark Lands.

"Well, well," Granny Hedgepath said. "Whom do I see but Mollie Cloverall from Lower Hexham."

I stared at her, speechless with surprise.

She laughed and came close enough for me to smell her familiar odor of smoke and damp earth and herbs. "What's wrong, girl? Cat got your tongue?"

"Granny," I stammered. "What are you doing here?" For the first time ever, I was glad to see her.

"Why, you never know where I'll turn up," she said. "I'm a wanderer, I am. I go here and there and everywhere."

Guest squeezed my hand as if he was scared.

"You remember Granny," I said to him. "She lives

on the other side of Cat Tail Hill, not far from Mam and Dadoe."

He said nothing, but his face screwed up like he smelled something bad. Ducking behind my skirt, he peered at her. Granny had that effect on people, I thought, scaring them with her strange ways and words, but meeting her here in the Dark Lands seemed good luck. Perhaps she'd seen something that would help us.

"You done what you said you'd do," Granny said. "I thought it were a foolish boast from a foolish girl, but here you be far from home, and it still with you."

"I've not found the Kinde Folke yet. Do you know where they hide themselves?"

"Indeed, I do. They been helping me find my roots and berries." She held up the basket she carried, and I saw a heap of dead plants.

Her wrinkled face split into a grin. "Come with me, the two of you, and I'll take you to them."

"Did you see Thomas? Is he well?"

"Oh, he's very well, indeed. Those ones take good care of him. Yes, they do."

"And I've taken good care of Guest. See how he's grown? He walks and talks now. He—"

"Oh yes," she cut in. "But he's what he is, ain't he? And always will be."

She spat on the ground almost at Guest's feet. "You done wasted your time dragging him along with you. They got no use for his kind."

I held Guest's hand tighter. "Will the Kinde Folke give me Thomas?"

"Well, you just come along with me, Mollie. I'll take you straight to the queen herself, and she'll give you Thomas. Yes, indeed, she will, oh yes, indeed." Granny laughed and clapped her hands.

Guest whimpered and tugged at my skirt. Embarrassed, I swatted his hands away. "Don't be rude, Guest. Say hello to Granny, show her how much you've learned."

Guest hid his face in my skirt and said not a word.

Granny laughed. "He ain't no different. Just bigger." She reached for my hand. "Come along with me if you want to see Thomas. I ain't got all day."

Guest tried to pull me away from Granny. I bent to look at his face. "What is wrong with you?"

He shook his head and pointed at Granny.

The old woman laughed again. "He don't like me, do he?"

"He's just tired, as I am. We've come so far."

"That you have, but come, come along with me. Soon you'll have your Thomas and be rid of that one and be on your way home."

With Guest trying to hold me back, I trudged into the ferns after Granny. "How is Mam?" I asked her. "And Dadoe, did he come back? Do they miss me? Are they worried?"

"Hush, child, everyone is fine. Your father's home and your mother's a-blooming with health. Happy they are that the changeling is gone. But sad to lose both their children."

I took Guest's hand and tried to tow him after me, but he dug his heels into the earth and refused to move. "It's all right," I whispered to him. "She's taking us to the Kinde Folke. Be nice, Guest."

Granny smiled at me. I'd never noticed what a foxy grin she had. Perhaps I'd not seen a smile on her grumpy face before now.

"Thomas will be right happy to see you, Mollie. That he will. And the Kinde Folke, too. Such a brave girl to come all this way. Yes, indeed. They got a grand feast all ready for you . . ."

It was odd, but the more Granny talked, the less I

understood. Her words had become a stream of water running over smooth stones, soothing but senseless.

After what seemed miles, we came to a hollow in the ferns. Granny's endless talking had made me dizzy. I swayed on my feet, feeling as if I could barely stand.

"Oh, dear me, Mollie, look at you, about to topple over." Granny helped me sit down in the ferns. "Rest you right here. I'll go fetch Thomas."

Before she left, she took a pretty little blue bottle out of her basket. "This is my elixir of health," she said. "Drink it and you'll soon feel fit to greet Thomas."

I took the bottle eagerly, thirstier than I'd ever been in my life. "Thank you," I whispered.

"I'll be back in a trice." With a laugh, Granny disappeared into the ferns.

I pulled out the stopper and lifted the bottle to my lips, but before I took one sip, Guest leapt out of the ferns and knocked the bottle out of my hand. Its contents poured onto the ground. Although Guest tried to shoo it away, a butterfly dipped down to drink from the puddle of elixir. In a moment, it lay still and the ferns around it withered.

I stared at the dead butterfly, my head spinning with

thirst. "Surely Granny never meant to poison me. The Kinde Folke must have tricked her."

Guest shook his head. "She not Granny. Kinde Folke magic."

"Why didn't you tell me?"

He pointed to his mouth. "Granny taken my words. I pulled you, I tugged, I made faces, but . . ." He shrugged.

I bowed my head and started to cry. "Oh, Guest, I believed her, I thought she'd bring Thomas. I was sure she would."

He began pulling and tugging at me again. "Not safe here. We go back to path."

Staggering to my feet, I ran with Guest, but the path wasn't where we thought it should be. In growing fear, we pushed through tall grasses and stumbled into bogs, sinking ankle-deep, sometimes knee-deep before we pulled our feet free. We made our way through clumps of heather that clung to our ankles and tripped us. I lost my walking stick and almost left a boot in a bog. Strange voices called our names. Muffled by dense gray air, they seemed to surround us, but we couldn't tell where they came from or how close they were. Midges with bites as sharp as the Tinies' teeth swarmed around us.

Just when I thought I couldn't take another step, Guest cried out, "Mollie, the path, the path. I see it!"

I stumbled out of the woods behind Guest. The white stones bordering the path glowed softly in the dusk. The voices calling us faded into the distance. For now, at least, we were safe.

9

WE SLEPT BADLY THAT night, hiding ourselves as best we could under a ledge of rock. In the morning, we went on, our bodies stiff and weary, our bellies empty.

The land around us was studded with boulders and tall rock formations, dull and gray. Not a village, not a farmhouse, not a man, woman, or child to be seen. No birds. No animals. Not even a breeze to stir the air. Just Guest and me. Alone in the Dark Lands.

Days and nights, nights and days, streamed past like leaves blown in the wind. I'd lost count of them long ago. It seemed as if we'd been walking for a week, a month, a year, a hundred years. Like everything in this land, time moved to different laws. Nothing seemed fixed or certain.

There were times when I was no longer sure of anything —not even Guest. I could not think who he was or why we were here and not at home with Mam and Dadoe. Or if Mam and Dadoe still existed. Or had ever existed.

After days or maybe weeks of walking, we stopped to rest by a stream. We'd been eating frogs and fish we caught in streams, berries, and sometimes a rabbit or a squirrel Guest managed to trap. Guest was so skinny, I could count his ribs.

We were tired and weak from hunger, but the stream's mossy bank was quiet and peaceful. Soon the sound of water running over stones lulled us both to sleep. I woke from a dream of home and almost wept to see the dark forest instead of sunlit fields. Guest was still sleeping, so I lay where I was, listening to the running water. *Rest while you can,* I told myself.

Gradually I became aware of another sound. At first, I thought it was the wind moving through the trees, but, as I listened, I realized it was a baby's cry. I got to my feet to hear better. Yes, it was a baby lost in the forest and crying for help.

"Thomas," I whispered. "Thomas, is it you?"

The baby cried louder. Leaving Guest asleep, I crept into the forest. If I woke him, he'd try to stop me, he'd say it was another trick, but I was certain Thomas had escaped somehow from the Kinde Folke and was trying to find his way home.

When I was far enough away to be sure of not waking

Guest, I called softly, "Thomas, where are you? It's me, Mollie. I've come to take you home."

The bushes rustled and a baby crawled toward me. His blond curls were tangled and his rosy face was pale and dirty, but it was Thomas, laughing and stretching out his hands to me.

I lifted him up in my arms and hugged him. "Oh, Thomas, I've missed you so."

He smiled and cooed and touched my face. "Mollie, Mollie."

"You can say my name now," I whispered. "Oh, Thomas, you remember me."

Holding my brother safe in my arms, I told him about the long journey I'd taken to find him. "I'll bring you to Guest, and then we'll start for home. Oh, you can't imagine how happy Mam and Dadoe will be."

Joyfully, I carried my brother through the forest, looking for the place where I'd left Guest. Wouldn't he be surprised when he saw whom I'd found? Why, we could go home without ever meeting the Kinde Folke.

I didn't think I'd gone far, but I walked and walked without finding the stream. I passed the same tree twice before

I realized I was going in circles. Like everything else in the Dark Lands, the path changed every time I left it, meandering this way and that.

With every step I took, Thomas grew heavier. But how could I complain? It was my own sweet brother I carried, the baby I'd almost lost through my own foolishness, the baby I'd soon bring home to Mam and Dadoe.

But I was weak from hunger, tired, and thirsty, and I was stumbling over stones and roots. I feared I'd fall with Thomas in my arms and hurt him. When I saw a mossy spot by a tall oak tree, I sank to the ground.

"Oh, Thomas," I whispered. "I'm so weary. Let's sit and rest for a moment."

Holding him on my lap, I sang a lullaby Mam used to sing. He leaned against me, his head heavy on my shoulder.

"Do you remember this song, Thomas? Mam sang it to you and to me as well. Soon we'll both be safe at home, and she'll sing it while she rocks you to sleep in your own cradle."

I smiled down at him. He stared at me through half-closed eyes. He didn't smile. His face was different somehow, not as round as I'd thought, and not as sweet.

Fearing he was ill, I hugged him and kissed the top of his

head. "Are you sick? Does something hurt? Have the Kinde Folke treated you badly? Mam will make everything all right—she'll feed you and bathe you and love you."

I didn't expect Thomas to answer my questions, but I was surprised by the low angry sound he made, almost like a growl it was. His body tensed and lost its softness.

I held him tighter. "Please don't be angry with me, Thomas. It's all my fault they took you, and I'm heartily sorry I was so careless. I'll never let you out of my sight again, I promise."

He struggled to escape, and when I tightened my hold on him, he snarled and sunk his teeth into my arm. Shocked, I let him go. His lips drew back and exposed long, sharp teeth. Fur covered his body. What crouched in front of me was a wolf, not Thomas.

I drew back in horror, but the wolf lunged at me and knocked me to the ground. He stood over me, teeth bared, and growled. I'd seen wolves before but never one like this. From where I lay, he seemed the size of a horse. His teeth were the longest and sharpest I'd ever seen. And his eyes—they were cruel beyond belief. He meant to kill me, and I was too weak with fear to try to escape.

He spoke to me in a rough and raspy voice. "You will not

see your brother. You will not rescue him. You will not take him home. He is lost to you and your parents."

"Please, please," I begged, "have mercy. Thomas is ours—you stole him from us."

"You ask a wolf for mercy?" He opened his mouth wide and grinned, showing me his teeth again. "Thomas is ours, not yours. You should not have come to this land. I am here to see that you never leave it."

Using my heels to push against the earth, I tried to stand, but I was too weak.

He grinned, and on his breath, I smelled places not known to me. I could not imagine what he'd seen, what he'd done.

"What do you have to say, girl?"

Even if I'd had something to say, my mouth was too dry with fear to speak.

But perhaps there was something else I could do. As he leaned over me, poised to attack, I pulled out the locket and pressed it as hard as I could against one of his eyes. With a savage howl, he leapt backwards, one eye gone, nothing left of it but a smoking hole and the stench of burned flesh.

I had no idea which way to go, but I ran away from the wolf. Behind me, he continued to howl, but he didn't come after me. Maybe he was in too much pain. Maybe he was calling his brothers. All I knew to do was to keep running.

When I couldn't take another step, I collapsed under a tree. Gripping the locket, I waited for my heart to slow. I gasped for breath. My side ached, and my legs shook. The Kinde Folke had tricked me again. They knew I'd not turn down a chance to rescue Thomas and carry him home to Mam.

I looked at the bite mark on my arm. It had stopped bleeding, but blood stained my dress all the way down to its hem.

Wearily I got to my feet and began to search for the path again. Once more voices called to me from the shadows; once more I stumbled and fell and wandered through bogs and heather, wolves howling somewhere behind me.

When I'd all but given up, I stumbled onto the path and saw Guest running toward me, his skinny legs pumping hard.

"Where you been? I wake up and you was gone. Why did you leave? Madog said—"

"I know what Madog said, but I heard Thomas crying, and I went to find him. I picked him up, but I couldn't find the path. Then Thomas turned into a wolf. I put out his eye with the locket and ran away. I ran and I ran and I ran."

He patted my arm to comfort me and saw the bite mark and the blood. "Mollie, you bleed, you hurt."

"The wolf bit me. I need to clean it."

Guest led me to the stream, and I washed the bite as best I could. It began to bleed again, but I found a weed I'd seen Mam use for healing. I mashed the stem and smeared it on the wound. Then I tore off part of my skirt and washed the cloth in the stream. Guest tied it around my arm.

We walked until night fell and camped in a cave by a stream. Guest caught a couple of fish, more bone than anything else. After we ate them, we sat by the fire together, fearing every sound we heard. In the distance, a wolf howled, then another. I shivered and threw more wood on the fire.

In the dark spaces between the trees, a twig snapped, and Guest drew closer to me. "Something there."

"It's them again with a new trick." I stared into the dark, weary beyond weary. What would they do this time? Did I have the strength to face them again?

Another twig snapped, nearer to us. I pulled the locket out of my dress and held it up so the silver caught the firelight. "Who's there?"

"Who wants to know?"

Brandishing the locket, I said, "I want to know."

A boy stepped into the firelight. His face was dirty, his hair a black tangle of knots and snarls, and his clothes were as faded and ragged as mine. "You must be Mollie."

"Who are you, and how do you know my name?" Curling my fingers tightly around the locket, I dared him to come closer. "And don't tell me any of your fine lies, for I know the ways of your people."

"You know nothing of me nor the ways of my people. Indeed, I know more of you than you know of me. A simpleton you are, Mollie Cloverall."

Whoever this boy was, he had no right to speak so rudely. "I don't know who's been spreading lies about me, but I'm no simpleton. This locket I hold—"

"I've already been told about the locket. The silver hides the iron underneath. Don't threaten me with it."

I studied him in the firelight. He wasn't more than a year or two older than myself and not even an inch taller. Though he didn't look dangerous, I didn't trust him. "Tell the truth," I said. "Why are you here?"

"Someone sent me with a message for you."

"Oh, no, I'll not fall for that trick again." I thrust the locket toward him. "Go back to the Kinde Folke and tell them Mollie Cloverall has come to fetch her brother home."

The boy stepped back and held out his hands, palms toward me as if to fend me off. "Keep that bauble away from me," he said. "I'm not one of them, but my people have dealings with those ones from time to time. Cheats and thieves, they are. Wicked, too. Bargains made and bargains broken. Truth told at midnight turns to lies before sunrise."

A thought came to me. Maybe it was the way the boy spoke or the way he held his head. "Who are you? Did Madog send you?"

"I'm Aidan, Madog's son. He made me come."

"Madog never spoke of having a son. How do I know you're telling the truth?"

Aidan shrugged and spread his hands just as I'd seen Madog do. "You'll have to take my word for it, won't you?"

Still suspicious, I eyed him closely. Sure enough he looked like Madog. "Why didn't Madog himself come?"

"Oh, *he* has important business," Aiden said. "And *I*, of course, have nothing to do except obey his orders, even when they are daft."

I dropped the locket inside my dress. This boy was ill-natured but not a threat. "Truth to tell," I said, "I wish Madog had come and left you at home."

"And so do I." Aidan dropped his bag and stretched. He looked at Guest, who had said not a word but stood staring at Aidan.

"I've never seen one of his sort before," Aidan said. "If they're all as ugly as he is, it's no wonder folks leave them to starve at crossroads."

The boy had a vexing way about him, and I disliked him more with every word he spoke. "Don't speak of him as if he can't understand what you say."

"Madog told me you brought the changeling with you all the way from Lower Hexham. You have some idea the Kinde Folke will trade him for your brother."

"No, not anymore."

"What will you do with him, then?"

I looked at Guest. He'd gathered sticks and stones and was sorting them by size and shape. What was I going to do with him?

"I'd leave him here," Aidan said. "And be glad to see the end of him."

Guest had begun building a stone tower. He didn't speak or look up, but I knew he was listening.

"I can't just leave him in this awful place," I said. "I guess I'll take him home with Thomas and me."

"Oh, your parents will love that."

"Maybe not right away," I said, "but in the end they'll take him in."

"In the end?" Aidan laughed. "Not ever, I say."

Guest looked at Aidan and began to speak in the language he and Madog shared.

Aidan made a short reply in the same language.

Guest whimpered and drew closer to me.

In anger, I turned to Aidan. "What did you say to him?"

Aidan folded his arms across his chest. "Why should it matter to you?"

I couldn't say when or why, but I had begun to care about Guest. I couldn't bear to see Aidan treat him as if he had no feelings. "You had no cause to be mean to him," I said. "He was only being friendly."

"I told him the truth, that's all. I'll never be a friend to a changeling." Aidan spit on the ground at my feet. "I hate the creatures."

"What has a changeling ever done to you? You just said you'd never even seen one before."

"I have a mind to leave you here and go home to my mam's cottage."

"Well, why don't you? Guest and I have no need of you."

"You need this, I wager." Aidan opened his pack and dumped out cheese and bread and apples. "It's from Madog, not me. You and the changeling can starve for all I care."

My stomach was too empty to spurn the food. Instead of leaving, Aidan set about making a fire. I toasted the bread on a stick and melted the cheese on top.

Aidan ate with us, but he cast a cloud over the meal. No one spoke. We simply filled our bellies.

Guest sat close to me. Every now and then, I caught him looking at Aidan, his face fearful.

"Don't mind him," I whispered. "He's rude and dirty, but he's Madog's son. He can't be all bad."

Guest looked at me with mournful eyes. "You won't leave me here?"

"You heard what I told Aidan. You and Thomas will go home with me. I promise."

"But them at your house want Thomas, not me. They won't let me stay."

"When Mam and Dadoe see how much you've changed, they'll be glad to keep you."

Guest plainly doubted Mam and Dadoe would treat him kindly. Much as I hated to admit, I wasn't so sure myself.

Aidan spoke up from his side of the fire. "Go to sleep. We've a hard walk ahead of us."

Guest fell asleep almost at once, but I watched Aidan through half-closed eyes. I believed he was watching me, too. I didn't trust him, and he didn't trust me. If only Madog was sleeping on the other side of the fire and Aidan was far away.

The next day passed in the usual way—perilous climbs up and down rocky hills, rain in our eyes, wind buffeting us, midges biting us. It was a weary business, and my legs burned with the effort to keep up with Aidan. Guest clung to my hand and slowed me down. Every now and then, Aidan stopped and waited for us, clearly impatient.

A fierce wind gave voices to the trees around us. Tossing and swaying, limbs creaking and groaning, they seemed to say, *Turn back. Leave this land. You don't belong here. You aren't wanted.*

With Aidan in the lead, I struggled up a steep hill, dragging Guest behind me.

"Bad place," he muttered over and over again.

"Hush, you're scaring me," I told him.

He looked at me, shook his head, and said no more. But his lips moved, and I suspected he was still telling himself we were in a bad place.

Near the top of the hill, I stopped behind Aidan. Above us, a ring of tall stones thrust up from the earth. Their tops vanished into a heavy mist. In their center lay a massive slab of rock like a stage or an altar. Strong magic hung heavy in the air. I breathed it in and felt it burn my lungs. It crawled across my skin and prickled my scalp. I wanted to run back down the hill, but fear rooted me to the earth.

Guest squeezed my hand so hard, I felt my bones shift. He breathed fast, his bony chest rising and falling as fast as a baby bird's.

"I thought their home was miles away," Aidan said, "yet here it is. Madog should be with us. He—"

As he spoke, green flames raced across the ground toward us. My skin tingled and my hair crackled. Guest and Aidan glowed as if they were burning from within.

The flames vanished as quickly as they'd come, and a terrible silence fell. It was as if the green light had swallowed up every sound and nothing would ever be heard again. Not a bird, not a human voice.

In that silence, a woman in a long green cape stepped into the center of the stone circle. Head thrown back, she stood with her arms lifted to the sky as if she were calling lightning down on all of us. She shone with a light so dazzling, I couldn't look at her.

Aidan fell to his knees. Guest and I did the same. We all bowed our heads and waited for her to speak.

"Two children and a changeling," the lady said at last. "How pitiful." She paused a moment. "Stand up, come closer, let me see the miserable creatures I've trapped in my circle."

With fear and hesitation, I got slowly to my feet and pulled Guest up with me. He shook so hard, he almost fell at the lady's feet. Pale-faced, Aidan stood a few feet away. He looked past the lady's shoulder, into the gloom behind her. I did the same, thinking it must be the proper thing to do.

Guest pressed his head against my side and didn't look at anything. He clutched my dress so tightly, I feared he'd tear it.

"Boy," she said to Aidan. "Come to me."

Aidan stumbled forward. "Your Majesty," he whispered, but before he spoke another word, the lady struck his face with her open hand. Aidan's head snapped back, and he raised an arm to protect himself from a second blow.

"Do not speak to the queen until she tells you to." Her voice was so calm, I scarcely believed she'd just struck Aidan hard enough to make him stagger.

"I know who you are and why you are here," she went on in that same level voice. "If I allow you to live, and I'm not yet certain I will, tell Madog not to send a boy when a man is needed. Tell him I am angry that he has helped your contemptible companions to come this far into my land. He cannot protect them from my wrath."

She paused a moment. I felt rather than saw the queen direct her gaze from Aidan to Guest and me.

"Impertinent, foolish girl," she said, "do you truly believe I will return your brother?"

Was I expected to answer the question, or would I, too, receive a slap?

The air stirred before I felt the blow. Stumbling backwards, I almost knocked Guest down. He whimpered and held my skirt tightly.

"Answer the queen when she asks a question," she said sweetly.

"Your Majesty." I looked directly at the queen, but in the bright light shining from her, I couldn't make out her features. "My mother is wasting away with grief, and my father has left us. I have come a long way to beg you to be as kind as you are beautiful and allow me to take Thomas home."

The queen laughed. "Such a pretty speech. How amusing you are." Turning to the crowd gathered behind her, she said, "Bring the boy forth. Let him decide whether to go or stay."

I could scarcely believe how easily I'd won. All smiles and laughter, Thomas would stretch out his arms to me. Once again I'd hold him and smell the sweet baby scent of him. I'd bring him home and see Mam smile. I took a deep breath and searched for my brother in the crowd behind the queen.

The Kinde Folke nudged one another and hid laughter behind their hands. In the rear, hidden from sight, a child protested angrily. People stepped aside to clear a space for a young Kinde One, a girl about my age. She dragged a boy seven or eight years of age behind her. His face was pale as if he seldom saw the sun, and he wore a blue velvet suit trimmed with lace and fastened with gold buttons.

"Why have you brought me here?" he asked the girl. "Let me go now, or I'll give you a kick you won't soon forget."

The girl stepped back, but she didn't release him. "It's the queen's order," she told him. "You must stand still and answer a question."

He saw the queen then and smiled. "Of course, Your Majesty. I will do as you bid."

Despite his blond curls and pretty face, I disliked him on sight. He was ill-tempered and rude.

"I present Prince Tiarnach," the queen said. "Curtsy to him, Mollie."

While the boy smiled scornfully, I bent my knees clumsily. "Where is Thomas? You said—"

The queen took the sulky boy's hand and smiled at me. "Why, Mollie my dear, do you not recognize your brother, the one you've come so far to find?"

I looked at the boy. Although he resembled Thomas somewhat, he was a boy, not a baby. It was another Kinde Folke trick, another lie.

"You seem puzzled, dear," the queen said. "Is this not your brother?"

"Of course not. Thomas is a baby."

The queen laughed and the others joined in, but the boy scowled.

"I assure you, this is the brother you seek. Shame on you not to recognize him."

"You're playing a trick on me."

"Don't try my patience, Mollie. If you do not believe this boy is your brother, leave my land and do not return."

Still filled with doubt, I looked at the boy. His blond curls, his blue eyes. Time ran differently here. Maybe it was indeed my brother standing before me.

I hesitated. "Thomas, don't you remember me?"

The boy drew himself up as straight and tall as he was able. "My name is Tiarnach, not Thomas. I have no sister. Take my advice and leave our land."

Bewildered, I said, "You are my brother. My mother is your mother, and my father is your father. Come home with me, and you'll see how much we love you."

I stepped toward him, but he backed away as if I carried the plague.

"This land is my home," he said. "I know no other land. I do not know you." Scorn frosted his eyes, and his voice was as cold as the queen's. "Leave here at once, and tell me no more lies."

"Your home is on the farm with Mam and Dadoe and me. Not here. These are not your people. They are—" I clapped my hand over her mouth to avoid saying the Kinde Folke's true name. "They have cast a spell on you!"

The queen swept toward me. The hem of her long silken gown hissed behind her. At last, I saw her face. Skin as white as foam at the foot of a moonlit waterfall, hair as dark as a cavern so deep the sun never shines there, eyes as green as priceless jewels, features as delicate as if she'd been carved from ivory by a sculptor of rare skill.

But behind that perfect face was something dark and inhuman. I backed away, not so much from fear as from caution. The people of this land were even more dangerous than I could have imagined. And this one, the queen standing before me, was the most dangerous of all.

The queen's lips curled upward at the corners, but it wasn't a smile I saw. "You'd best be on your way, dear Mollie. Tiarnach is happy with us." Her smile froze my skin. "What a pity to come so far and return empty-handed."

The queen turned to Guest with a sneer. "Take this filthy

toad with you, unless you wish to leave him here to die in the forest—which would be for the best."

As she spoke, I felt Guest's heart beat fast and hard against my side.

I forced myself to meet her eyes, although it was all I could do not to turn away. "I won't leave until you release my brother from the spell you've cast upon him. Then I'll take both him *and* Guest home with me and never bother you again."

Aidan turned his head away as if he couldn't bear to see what would happen next.

The queen simply shook her head. "My, my, Mollie, what a foolish child you are. Normally I'd order my guards to kill you for such impertinence, but come now, I'm curious. How else will you entertain me? Tell me. I've never met such a comical fool."

My knees shook, and I held Guest's hand as tightly as he held mine. "You may laugh, but I love my brother, and I will take him from you."

Turning to Thomas, the queen said, "What say you, Tiarnach?"

Thomas drew himself up proudly. "This is my land," he said again. "I will not go with her."

The Kinde Folke laughed and vanished into the dusk. The sky turned black, and the wind rose into a roar. The tall stones seemed to grow even taller. They tilted and bowed and whirled around us as if they danced to the wind's music, creaking and groaning with every movement.

"Thomas," I cried. "Thomas!"

But he was gone. Still holding Guest's hand, I fell with him into a dark, cold, silent place where nothing moved.

10

I OPENED MY EYES TO find myself lying on the mossy ground at the foot of the tallest stone in the circle. It towered over me like a robed figure from a dimly remembered story, dark and foreboding.

Guest squatted beside me, stroking my face with his cold hands. "Mollie, wake up, wake up," he begged.

Aidan stared down at us. "On your feet," he said. "This is no place to linger."

Without any help from Aidan, I struggled to stand. My legs ached with fatigue, and I was weak and dizzy. The Kinde Folke had gone and taken Thomas with them, leaving no trace of themselves behind.

Clinging to Guest's hand to steady myself, I followed Aidan slowly down the hill, trying not to slip on the damp, mossy stones. How long had I lain unconscious? Was it dusk or dawn? It was impossible to tell. The gray light and misty rain cast a perpetual twilight in the woods.

Once we were on the path, Aidan found shelter in a shallow cave and set about making a fire. Guest and I huddled together and watched the flames sputter on the wet wood.

"What should I do now?" I asked.

Aidan didn't bother to look at me. Frowning into the fire, he said, "You heard what *she* said. Go home. Your brother's not of a mind to leave the Kinde Folke. The longer we stay here, the more the danger."

Aidan laid two potatoes on the fire.

"You need to roast another," I said. "There's three of us."

"I count two. Me and you."

"You've left out Guest."

"Why should I cook for him?"

Taking a third potato from the sack, I laid it beside the other two. I half expected Aidan to remove Guest's potato, but he left it where I'd put it.

After we'd eaten our potatoes and what was left of the apples, cheese, and bread, I heard a noise in the dark beyond the firelight. Alarmed, I looked at Aidan, but he was already on his feet.

"Where have you been?" he shouted. "The Kinde Folke near killed us all."

Madog stepped out of the woods. "I didn't know how close you were to the stones. It's glad I am to see all of you unharmed."

With a smile at Guest and me, he turned to Aidan, and the two spoke together in low voices.

Madog shook his head, frowned, and then sat down beside me. "Aidan tells me you were less than courteous to Her Royal Kindeness. Why must you speak your mind without giving a thought to what you say? If the queen hated you before she met you, she hates you even more now."

Aidan glanced at me. "I doubt anyone has ever spoken to the queen as that saucepot did. Someone should stuff a rag in her mouth. She's made things worse for us all."

"What did you do to help?" I asked. "Nothing, nothing at all. You stood there and watched, even after she hit you. You don't care what happens to Thomas or me or anyone else."

"And why should I care? Your brother can stay or go, it's all the same to me. And the toad—"

"Enough, Aidan," Madog said. "It shames me to hear you speak so."

Aidan poked at the fire, his face lit by the flames. He said nothing, but anger steamed from him.

Guest sat down beside Madog. "I miss you. I happy you back."

Madog grinned and looked him up and down. "You've grown," he said, and leaned closer to speak softly to Guest in the language they shared.

I sat alone and stared at the glowing odds and ends of the fire. I was tired, so tired, of living like a traveler with no bed of my own and no roof over my head, always hungry, always cold, always wet from rain and fog. This was a dreadful place, and I was sick to death of it.

Madog leaned toward me. "Such a sad little face you have. Surely you've not given up hope."

I fidgeted with the locket, turning it this way and that, watching it catch the light of the fire. "Thomas wants to stay with the Kinde Folke, where he is a prince." I sniffled and rubbed my eyes, determined not to cry, but a tear escaped and another one followed, and soon they were running down my cheeks and my chest was heaving with sobs.

"Perhaps Aidan is right," Madog said. "Since Thomas

wants to stay, perhaps you should let him. If we sneak away tonight, we might escape the wrath of the Kinde Ones."

"You know I can't do that. I must bring Thomas home to Mam and Dadoe."

Aidan spoke up from the other side of the fire. "The half-wit will be the death of us all."

I jumped to my feet. "If you hate me and Guest so much, why don't you leave? We don't need you now that Madog is here."

"I say you and me both should be on our way," Aidan said to Madog. "You have business to attend to, and there's a certain lass waiting for me."

Madog looked long and hard at Aidan. "My business will wait," he said, "and so will your lass."

Aidan lay down with his back to the fire. Guest was asleep under his blanket. Madog and I were the only ones awake.

"Why does Thomas want to stay here?" I asked him. "Why doesn't he remember me? Has the queen cast a spell on him?"

Madog gazed into the dark forest where no light shone, not even moonlight. "Thomas has lived in her kingdom so long he remembers no place else. Spell or no spell, he believes he's one of the Kinde Folke now."

"He was a baby when they took him. Why does he look older than he is?"

"Surely you've heard tales of mortals who join the Kinde Folke for a night of dancing and wake to find themselves old men in a changed world."

Yes, of course I'd heard those stories, but I'd never known such a thing to happen in real life. I looked down at myself. Was my dress a little tighter now? Certainly my hair was longer. "Am I older than I was when I left home?"

Madog shook his head. "You must bide with those ones in their dwellings to feel time as they do."

I sat back, relieved. For how was I to know? I'd no mirror to look in to. And just as well, I thought, for I was dirty and ragged, and my hair was a tangled mess. I wouldn't care to see my reflection.

"But Guest—he's bigger than he was when we started," I said.

"He grows at his own pace, faster than you it seems." He smiled. "And glad you should be, for how could you have carried him all this way?"

Madog turned his attention to Aidan. "Get up and make yourself useful," he said. "Fetch all the wood you can carry.

You know as well as I the value of fire on a dark night in a dark land."

Long after Aidan had vanished among the trees, I heard him crashing through the bushes, a sure sign he was still angry.

"Why do we need wood?" I asked Madog. "We always let the fire go out at night."

"Did I not say you're in danger here?" Madog asked. "We must build a ring of fire around us. None of their kind dare to cross over flames."

I shivered. "It's me they want, isn't it?"

"Mostly," Madog said. "But they don't care for Aidan or me, either. They detest Guest, but they can't harm him because he shares their blood. They simply leave his sort to die alone in the forest. Or they trade them for fine babies like Thomas."

Guest sighed in his sleep and snuggled closer to me. *Half Kinde Folke,* I thought, *and half what else?*

Madog touched Guest's head lightly. "I'll keep him safe, and you too. I promise."

I looked at the changeling's sleeping face. It shamed me to think how much I'd once hated him. In those days, I was no better than Aidan.

"Homely he is," Madog said. "But he's a spunky one, do you not agree?"

"Oh yes, indeed. He helped me chase away the Tinies and escape from Granny Hedgepath."

"Did he, now?"

"He did, but I saved my own self from False Thomas, the crying baby who changed into a wolf and tried to kill me."

"And how did you escape from the wolf?"

I pulled the locket from my dress and waved it in Madog's face. He scooted backwards so fast, he almost fell into the fire. His face dark with anger, he said, "Never do that again, Mollie. Do you hear? Never."

"Oh, please don't be angry. I'm sorry. I forgot."

"Try to remember the next time you reach for that locket. Use it on them, not me."

"What are you, Madog, that you fear the touch of iron? You can't be one of them, but you and Aidan are not like me."

"I told you. I'm a traveler."

"But what are travelers?"

I don't know what he would have said if Aidan hadn't come back with a huge armload of wood. He dumped it on the ground by the fire, which had almost burned itself out.

"I hope that's all you need, for it's not to my liking to stumble around the Dark Lands, hearing voices and strange sounds and almost losing my way."

Madog and Aidan laid the wood in a circle around our sleeping place. "A good fire will protect us from whatever the Kinde Folke send our way," Madog said.

When the fire burned strong and warm, Madog told Aidan to stay and tend it. "I'll collect more wood."

"What about her who's to blame for our plight?" Aidan asked, with another scowl at me. "Does she not collect wood too?"

"It's Mollie's place to watch Guest." Madog plunged into the shadows beyond the fire. He went as quiet as a deer and left no noise behind him.

Aidan sat at a distance from Guest and me. "How do you bear to be so close to that toad? Does not his stink fill your nose?"

"Why do you dislike Guest so much?" I asked.

Aidan spat into the fire. "Everyone despises his kind. Except you. And you are clearly a simpleton."

"Madog likes him."

Aidan spat again, harder this time, and the gob sizzled in the ashes. "He's a bigger fool than you are."

"Tell me something, Aidan." I wanted an answer, so I tried to speak like a grown woman, not a child to be lied to. "What are you and Madog? Who are your people? Where do you come from?"

Aidan poked a log back into the fire. "We're travelers from over the hills and far away."

"You're more than that."

"Ask Madog." Aidan rolled up in his blanket and turned his back on Guest and me.

Left to my own thoughts, I watched the fire. Smoke blew in my face and made my throat choky, but Guest slept on. Every now and then, his eyelids quivered as if he was dreaming. He grimaced, he moaned, he twitched, but he screwed his eyes tight shut and didn't wake.

"What is your other half?" I whispered. "A goblin? A troll?" I studied his face. Surely, he was none of these. Yet his father must have been a homely specimen, for Guest had not one speck of the Kinde Folkes' beauty.

When Madog returned, he carried enough wood to last

several days. I watched him build up the fire. When he seemed satisfied with its size, he glanced at Aidan. "Sound asleep," he muttered.

"I'm awake," I said.

Madog smiled and came to sit beside me. "What keeps your eyes open?"

"I'm wondering when they'll come and what they'll be and what they'll do."

Madog sniffed the wind. "We'll soon find out," he said. "They're already on the way."

I opened my mouth to ask my question again, but he raised his finger to his lips. "Something's coming. See the deer?"

As he spoke, a herd of deer burst out of the woods and ran past us, maybe ten, maybe more, their eyes wild in the firelight. I turned and watched their white tails vanish into the dark behind us. Two or three owls followed on silent wings. Then came badgers, foxes, and a bevy of small creatures, all as frightened as the deer.

"Animals know when danger's near," Madog said. "Storms, earthquakes, fires, Kinde Folke on the move."

I huddled beside him and waited, my breath shallow with fear. At first, I heard nothing, but gradually I became aware of rustling leaves and twigs snapping, heavy breathing, murmurs and whispers, a thickening of the darkness outside the ring of fire.

Gradually a shape emerged from the darkness, a man I thought, neither tall nor short, fat nor thin. Behind him were shadows that moved as trees would move if they were not rooted to the earth. Although I couldn't make out the man's face, his appearance was familiar, but it wasn't until he spoke that I knew him.

"Mollie," he called. "At last I've found you. Come, let me take you home."

I rose to my feet. My legs trembled. "Dadoe, how did you find me?"

"Oh, my poor dear child. You must be weary and cold and hungry." He stretched out his hand. "Come with me. Mam weeps for you and rues every unkind word she spoke."

Madog pulled me gently back from the fire's edge. "No, Mollie, it's a trick—like Granny Hedgepath and the wolf."

My whole self yearned to leap the fire and run to Dadoe. I'd missed him for so long, and there he stood—almost close enough to touch.

"Madog, you must believe me. It's no trick. I know my own

father when I see him." I struggled to free my hand from his, but he was much stronger than I was.

"Mollie, stay with me," he whispered. "Don't cross over the fire."

Another figure joined Dadoe. "Mam," I cried. "Mam." I struggled with all my might to free myself from Madog. "That's my mother!" I was crying now, fighting Madog with all my strength. "Mam. Mam!"

"Mollie," she called. "The Kinde Folke have given Thomas to us. We can go home now, all four of us, a family again."

Madog held me so tightly, my wrists felt numb. "You must see things for what they are. It's not your father or your mother, but two Kinde Ones glamorized to look like them."

"Do you think I don't know my own parents?"

My shouts woke Guest. He jumped up and grabbed my waist. "No, Mollie. Don't go! Trick, trick."

From beyond the flames, Mam cried, "Please, Mollie, we're here to take you and Thomas home. Do you not want to come with us?"

"Don't believe that traveler. He's a liar and a trickster," Dadoe said. "Be strong, daughter, break away from him, run to us."

My father was right. Madog was a liar and a trickster. My true parents had come for me. They had Thomas. I was going home. No one, not even Madog, could stop me.

In anger, I yanked the locket from around my neck and thrust it into Madog's face. With a cry of pain, he sprang back. I jumped the fire and ran toward my parents.

Behind me, Madog yelled, "The locket, hold fast to the locket. Save yourself!"

Mam and Dadoe waited with smiling faces and outstretched arms. "Dearest Mollie," they crooned. "Sweetest daughter. You'll be safe with us."

When I was almost close enough to touch Mam and Dadoe, I saw the shadows in the forest move and shift. I heard rustlings and whispers and the clink of metal.

In front of me. Mam and Dadoe slowly changed into a pair of Kinde Folke.

Horrified by my stupidity, I turned to run back to Madog and the fire, but dozens of Kinde Folke sprang out of the forest and formed a circle around me. They were beautiful, each and every one of them, man and woman both, but their eyes were cruel and their smiles wicked.

Terrified, I held up the locket, but they were too far away

to touch, and I was too frightened to move closer to them. "Stay away," I said. "I have iron."

Laughing, they joined hands and began to dance slowly around me. Moving in a strange rhythm of fast and slow steps, they chanted.

> *Cast away the locket*
> *Let the locket go*
> *Come, Mollie, come*
> *Cast away the locket*
> *Let the locket go*

As the Kinde Folke chanted, they danced faster until they became an endless spinning blur shining in the dark. Each flowed into the other as if they were one, not many.

My ears filled with their voices. I forgot my fear, I forgot the queen's angry face, I forgot Thomas, I forgot Mam and Dadoe and all that I'd ever known. Slowly my fingers lost their strength. My grip on the locket loosened. I grew dizzy, light-headed, tired.

The circle shrank; the dancers came closer. Closer. And closer. Their cloaks brushed against me like spiderwebs.

"Let the locket go," they crooned. "Let the locket go."

From far away, I heard Guest's voice on the wind, rising and falling. "Mollie, Mollie."

Coming to my senses, I caught the locket just as it began to fall from my hand. The dancers were close now, brushing against me, lost in their dance.

Lifting the locket high, I thrust it against their shoulders, their faces, their arms, their hands. The dancers screamed in pain; they broke the circle; they sprang apart. Safe from the locket at the forest's edge, they took a stand and cried out to me.

"Foolish mortal, you'll never see Tiarnach again!"

"He's ours now!"

"We'll burn your barn and your house."

"We'll kill your crops. We'll send plague to your village."

Still shouting threats, the Kinde Folke faded away into the darkness, but their threats hung in the air as if written in flames.

I leapt over the fire and fell to the ground, weeping tears of anger and pain. Guest knelt beside me and stroked my hair.

"Oh, Mollie," Madog said, "when will you learn?"

I forced myself to look at him. He was indeed angry, and I

lowered my head in shame. "The way they looked, the words they spoke—how was I to know what they really were?"

"Have you already forgotten Granny and the baby you thought was Thomas?"

Aidan looked across the fire at me. "Like most mortals, she sees what she wants to see."

I clutched Madog's arm. "They cannot do what they said, they—"

"Of course they can," Madog said. "And much more if they have a mind to. You have enraged them, Mollie. They will seek revenge against you and your people."

I heard Aidan snort scornfully.

"But, Madog—"

"Lie down." He spoke in a harsh voice I'd never heard him use. "Go to sleep. I've had enough of you for tonight."

"Sleep here, Mollie." Guest patted the ground beside him.

I lay next to him and took his hand. "You saved me," I whispered. "If you hadn't called my name, I'd have dropped the locket and they would have captured me."

Guest smiled. "I shout loud, a big shout. The shoutiest shout I ever made."

"Thank you. You're a good friend, Guest. Maybe my only friend tonight."

"Madog is mad now, but soon he won't be mad."

Guest yawned and curled up close to me. He drifted off to sleep, but I lay awake until almost dawn, afraid to close my eyes lest the flames die and the Kinde Folke return.

11

THE NEXT DAY CAME, dark as always and mizzling with rain and fog. I longed for sunlight and blue skies, for fields and meadows, for sheep on the hillsides as far as I could see, for larks singing over my head.

I looked for Madog, but he wasn't there. Neither was Aidan or Guest. I was alone by the dying fire.

"Madog," I called. "Aidan, Guest, where are you?"

The only answer came from a rook perched on a branch over my head. He cawed once, shifted his weight, and showered me with rainwater as he flew off.

Had my stupidity driven them all away, even Guest? What was I to do without them? Alone, I was no match for the Kinde Folke.

Kinde—I almost choked on the word. Those ones didn't know the meaning of kind. Hateful and merciless they were, as careless of mortal lives as if we were ants or flies—pests, vermin, things to destroy.

I hid my face in my hands and began to cry. I was lost, lost. I'd never see Thomas; I'd never find my way home; I'd be captured and die in this dark, miserable place.

If only I could go back to that day in the garden when I started all of this with careless words. I hadn't meant to call attention to Thomas, but even though I knew the locket protected him, I'd fastened it around my neck. If I hadn't done that, they couldn't have taken him.

I'd thought I could make everything right by persuading the Kinde Folke to give Thomas to me, but I'd failed miserably, stupidly, foolishly. I'd never get Thomas now. There was nothing to do but find my way home and beg Mam and Dadoe to forgive me. I lay on the cold ground by the dead fire and wept for all the mistakes I'd made.

"Mollie, get up." Guest pried my hands away from my face. "You cry?"

I sat up and hugged him so tightly, he squirmed to free himself. "I thought everyone left and I was all alone in the Dark Lands."

He held out Madog's hat filled with berries. "Look. I finded food for you."

I devoured the berries even though some of them weren't quite ripe. After I swallowed the last one, I felt better.

"Where is Madog?" I asked Guest.

"He and Aidan go for horses. We get away fast on horses. They run, run, run, faster, faster, faster!" Guest's voice rose, and he bounced up and down on his skinny legs. "I never rode a horse!"

"Hush," I whispered, "hush, calm yourself. We mustn't make too much noise. They might come again."

Guest pressed his finger to his mouth and grinned.

"Tell me," I said. "Is Madog still angry? Did he say anything about me?"

"Madog said to watch you and not let you do foolish thing."

I took that to mean Madog didn't have much faith in me. Well, I'd show him I wasn't as foolish as he thought. I'd stay right here with Guest and wait for him to return.

While we waited, I sat by the fire, and Guest squatted beside me building little towers out of stones. All around us, the woods were silent as if they were waiting too.

Suddenly Guest clutched my arm. "Mollie, listen. Someone comes. Not Madog, not Aidan."

A twig snapped with a tiny crack. A leaf moved like a whisper.

My hand went to the locket. Such a little thing it was. A bauble made of iron and coated with silver. But it had saved me last night. Jumping to my feet, I called, "Who's there?"

No one answered, no one stepped forth, but the ferns quivered as if something smaller than a man and bigger than a fox hid in their fronds.

Guest sniffed as if he were a dog. "Smell like Kinde Folke," he whispered.

I held up the locket. "Come out, we know you're there!"

After a few moments, a girl stepped from behind a tall oak. She wore the gray cloak of the Kinde Folke and blended into the mist.

She stopped when she saw the locket. "I mean you no harm," she told me in a low voice.

I would not be fooled again—not by a sweet voice or a pretty face. Brandishing the locket as if it were a flaming sword, I said, "Not a step closer!"

"Please trust me," she said. "I come in friendship."

Guest trembled, but I hid my fear. "Trust you? No, I will not. I know full well the tricks your kind play."

The girl pointed at Guest. "He's what I've come to see." She ran her eyes over him. "'Tis no wonder my mother took Tiarnach and left the changeling in his place."

"Your mother didn't just take my brother—she *stole* him."

The girl put on a haughty face. "The Lady Duatha did not steal your brother. She made a trade. Her baby for your mother's baby."

"A trade is something two people agree to, but my mother knew nothing of the so-called trade until it was done and Thomas was gone. Your mother is a thief, and you know it."

"Truly you have less sense than an acorn newly fallen from a tree. If Lady Duatha learns you called her a thief, you will regret speaking ill of her."

I swung the locket at the girl, and she jumped back. "Do not touch me with that, I beg of you."

I swung the locket closer to her face. "Tell me who you are and why you're here. And do not lie."

"My name is Aislinn, daughter of Lady Duatha. Although it shames me to admit it, the changeling is my half-brother. That's why I wanted to see him."

"If you've come to take him, I won't let you. He's *my* friend. And I'm not ashamed to say it."

"You're more than welcome to him. He's neither a Kinde One nor a traveler, but something in between. A misfit that belongs nowhere."

I looked at Aislinn in surprise. "Guest's father is a traveler?"

"Do you not know who his father is? Can't you guess?"

Guest had been building a tiny stone house for a green caterpillar he'd found, but when he heard his name, he looked up. "You know my dadoe?"

I looked at Guest and realized I must have known all along. Madog had given himself away from the very beginning—his kindness to Guest, the language they shared, the affection he showed.

Aislinn knew I'd figured it out. "My mother loved Madog. And he loved her. When the queen found out, she banned him from the Dark Lands. Such love is forbidden."

"Madog is my dadoe, my dadoe is Madog." Guest clapped his hands and laughed.

"My mother still has affection for Madog, maybe even love. It has softened her." Aislinn tossed her head as if she wanted me to know *she* wasn't soft. "My mother fears what the queen will do if she captures Madog. She also pities your brother."

"Why does she pity Thomas? He's happy here, so happy he wants to stay in the Dark Lands."

In a voice so low, I barely heard her, Aislinn said, "Tiarnach believes he will be our king, but we have not been completely truthful with him."

"That's no surprise," I said.

I waited for her to explain, but her words hung in the air like a bridge to nowhere.

I stepped closer to her. "What doesn't Thomas know?"

"Do you understand what a tithe is?"

"Of course I do. We pay a tithe to the lord of the estate whose fields we plow and plant and harvest. It's a tax—coins if we have them, but it can also be crops or a calf or a lamb. But what does tithing have to do with my brother?"

"Every seven years, we are sworn to give the Dark Lord of these lands a tithe. That's the price we pay to roam the world as free as the wind. Tonight is the Eve of Tithe. We will celebrate with my marriage to Tiarnach."

What she said was so ridiculous, I almost laughed. "How can you marry? Thomas is a child, and you're not much older than I am."

"Hear me out, Mollie, please. After the wedding ceremony, Tiarnach will be crowned king. He will rule for one day and then, and then . . ."

I waited for her to go on, but she stared at the ground as if she'd been struck speechless.

"What happens after that one day?" My words were ashes in my mouth. I dreaded her answer.

"Think, Mollie, do not force me to tell you."

"Tell me, I beg you, that Thomas is not the tithe. Even the Kinde Folke cannot be that wicked."

Aislinn looked down, as if ashamed to meet my eyes. "It's why he was taken. The bonniest boy in mortal land is the tithe that Cernunnos demands."

"This cannot be," I cried. "It must not be! The queen cannot be so heartless."

"Hush, Mollie, and listen to me. Tiarnach was a sweet baby before the Kinde Folke spoiled him with promises and baubles and clothes of velvet. He's become a foolish, prideful boy, but he does not deserve to be tithed to the Dark Lord. Nor do you and the others deserve the fate the queen has planned for you."

The air seemed to turn colder. "What is our fate?"

"After the wedding, the queen will lead the Wild Hunt. You and your companions will be her prey. No one escapes from her hounds and her horsemen. All of you will be captured and killed, and the changeling will be left to die in the forest."

I took a step away from Aislinn. No, it couldn't be true—it was too cruel, too wicked. I glanced at Guest to see if he'd heard, but he sat several feet away watching the caterpillar crawl up and down his arm.

"But my locket," I whispered. "It protects us from you. Just last night, I used it against a mob of Kinde Folke. They fled into the forest to escape it."

Aislinn shook her head. "The queen has powers far greater than your locket. Nothing you can do will stop her."

"What am I to do, then?"

"My mother and I have made a plan. We cannot promise it will work, and it will put you in great danger."

"Whatever it is, I will do it to save Thomas. Without him, I have no reason to go home."

Aislinn opened the bag she carried and pulled out a long

gray cloak much like the one she wore. "Duatha wove invisibility into every thread of this cloak. As long as you wear it, you can come and go as we do, no more than a shadow in the shadow of something else."

I took the cloak from her. It was as silky and light as milkweed fluff. Cautiously, I wrapped it around me.

"Cover your head. Don't let your face show."

I did as she said and turned to Guest. "Can you see me?"

He looked up from the little house and dropped the white stone he'd been about to add to it. "No! Off, take that off! Want to see you!"

I lowered the hood. "Here I am, silly."

"I don't like Kinde Folke magic! Bad."

"Don't fret, Guest. I won't do anything foolish." I stroked the cloak's soft fabric and turned to Aislinn. "It must be woven of cobwebs, mist, moonbeams, and secrets."

"Something of the sort, with a little magic mixed into the weaving of it." She looked into my eyes. "Listen closely and say if you can do what I tell you. It's the only way to save your brother."

Guest tugged at my skirt to get my attention. "No foolish thing. Give it back. Don't trust Kinde Folke. Madog—"

I twitched my skirt away from him. "Hush. Let Aislinn speak."

Aislinn spoke in a low voice. "When night falls, I'll come to you. Wear the cloak with the hood over your head so no one can see you. I'll lead you into the center of the stones. There I'll leave you and join Tiarnach at the high table."

Guest whimpered and pulled on my dress and begged me to wait for Madog to return.

I slapped his hands away. "Be quiet, Guest!"

Guest backed away from me. I wanted to apologize to him for the slap, which truly was more of a tap, but instead I waited for Aislinn to tell me the rest of the plan.

"Watch for me to give your brother a golden goblet. When he drinks, he will grow weary. As soon as he sleeps, approach from behind and wrap the cloak around him. Make sure you keep the hood on and stay hidden. Tiarnach will be too drowsy to struggle. Leave as quickly and as quietly as you can."

I tried to think of what might go wrong, but there were too many possibilities. So I said nothing and waited for Aislinn to tell me more.

"Make certain that Madog and Aidan are ready to depart the moment you return with Tiarnach. When the queen discovers he's gone, she will lead the Wild Hunt after you. Leave the Dark Lands as fast as you can. You won't be safe until you enter your own land. And maybe not even then. Her vengeance may follow you."

She paused a moment. "Can you do this, Mollie?"

"To save my brother, I'll do anything."

"Good. I'll return at nightfall." With that, she vanished into the trees. This time no twig snapped under her foot. No bush trembled. It was as if she'd never been there.

Guest frowned at me. "You hit me."

"I'm sorry I slapped your hands, but I had to listen to Aislinn, just as I must go with her tonight and do my best to save Thomas."

"Madog not like this. He won't let you go with her."

"Surely Madog will see I have no choice."

Guest shrugged. "Maybe, maybe not. But I say don't go."

He picked up the caterpillar and placed it inside the little stone house. Adding a leaf for a roof, he showed me the hole he'd made in one wall. "Door," he said. "So caterpillar can go outside."

I watched him make a pebble path from the door to a little fence he'd made of sticks. He was really clever with his hands. Maybe when we got home—*if* we got home—he'd help Dadoe fix things.

12

BEHIND US, MADOG STEPPED out of the woods almost as quietly as Aislinn had vanished. "Did I miss meeting a Kinde One just now?"

"She came to help me."

"*Help* you?" Madog stared at me. "How many times will you let them fool you? Do you never learn?"

"Don't be angry, Madog." I twisted the locket on its chain. "It was Aislinn. Her mother is Duatha—whom I think you know."

Madog's face flushed. "I know them both." For the first time since I'd met him, he seemed lost for words. He simply stood there, looking past me at the woods where Aislinn vanished.

"I telled Mollie not to talk," Guest said, "but she telled me hush. They maked a plan."

"A plan?" Madog looked at me. "Tell me all that Aislinn had to say."

I took a deep breath to keep my voice from shaking. "The Kinde Folke mean to give Thomas to the Dark Lord as their tithe."

"I suspected that might be the way of it."

"Duatha came up with a plan to save us all." I wrapped the cloak around me.

Madog cried out in surprise. I laughed and pulled the hood away from my face. "It's Duatha's gift of invisibility."

Guest scowled. "I telled you no more Kinde Folke tricks." With that, he turned to his caterpillar, which had crawled out of its new home. "You like leaf? You like grass?"

While Guest tried to feed the caterpillar, I described the plan. Madog listened closely, nodding, then frowning, then shaking his head, then nodding again.

"It might work," he said slowly. "But do you dare enter the circle by yourself, with no one to trust but Aislinn?"

I seized his arm. "Please, Madog, tell me I can do this thing."

"You're a brave girl, Mollie. If anyone can rescue Thomas, it's you." He got to his feet slowly. "It's getting late. I'll light a fire and roast the rabbits I caught."

Before we'd started eating, Aidan stepped out of the woods and joined us. "The horses are fed and tethered."

While we ate, I had little to say. My mind was fixed on rescuing Thomas. Aidan seemed to be in a better humor and talked quietly with Madog about the horses.

Guest moved closer and closer to Madog. When he was almost sitting in Madog's lap, he stared at him so hard that Madog finally noticed.

"What's on your mind, little lad?" he asked.

"Are you truly my dadoe? Truly?"

Madog laughed. "Indeed, I am. And glad am I to say it."

Aidan's good humor vanished. He tossed what was left of his dinner into the fire and stood up. "I'll see to the horses."

With that, he vanished into the woods. The horses greeted him with a chorus of whinnies, and he spoke to them in a pleasant voice I'd never heard him use.

Madog sighed and took Guest onto his lap. "Did Aislinn tell you?"

"Yes, but she told Mollie she was shamed of me."

Madog hugged him. "Never you mind what Aislinn says or Aidan either. Mollie loves you, and so do I."

Guest smiled.

By the time Aidan rejoined us, it was almost dark. Guest had fallen asleep, and Madog and I were talking quietly.

"What's your plan for tonight?" Aidan asked Madog. "You know they'll come again. In force this time."

"We'll have no company tonight," Madog said. "It's the Eve of Tithe, and they have a wedding to attend."

Aidan frowned. "I believe it's their custom to celebrate weddings with the Wild Hunt."

"By then we'll be gone from here."

"Without the boy? How did you get Mollie to agree to that?"

"Duatha sent her daughter with a plan to rescue Thomas."

Aidan scoffed. "Duatha—I want nothing to do with her or her plan. It's certain to be a trap."

Madog shrugged. "I trust Duatha."

Muttering to himself, Aidan walked away again. With his back to us, he stood silently at the edge of the forest.

Getting to my feet, I wrapped myself in the cloak and tiptoed to his side. Clearly unaware of me, Aidan muttered about Kinde Folke and changelings and treachery.

"Stop behaving like a half-wit mooncalf," I said.

Aiden looked right at me. "What sort of trick is this? I hear you, but I don't see you."

"I'm right here." I pulled the hood away from my face and laughed.

In wonder, Aidan touched the cloak. "This is Kinde Folke stuff. Where did you get it?"

"Aislinn gave it to me. I'll use it to rescue Thomas."

"You are even more foolish than I thought."

Madog took Aidan's arm and spun him around so they were face-to-face. "Listen to me, Aidan. There is a plan, a good one. Though it's dangerous for Mollie, she's agreed to it."

After Madog explained, Aiden shook his head. "You might be my father, but you're a fool to allow this girl to go anywhere with Aislinn."

"No one's asking you to go with me," I said.

Madog put his hand on Aidan's shoulder. "All you and I need to do is be ready to flee with Guest when Mollie returns with Thomas."

Aidan looked at his father in disbelief. "Have you lost your wits? The Kinde Folke will keep Thomas, and the Wild Hunt will capture us. Mollie will spend her mortal days as a slave. You and I will be tortured and killed, and the changeling will be left to die in the forest."

Madog scowled at his son. "Be quiet. No more of that talk."

"Duatha has bewitched you, for certain." Aidan's face reddened with anger. "Leave these ones to their fate, and come home to my mother. She demands it."

"Bronan has no right to give me orders."

Aidan turned away and stood apart. The day's gray light faded into shadows. The hoots of owls replaced the caws of crows and rooks. Gusts of wind swept through the trees and scattered the fire's coals. The dying flames lit the gleam of Madog's eye, the thrust of his nose, the line of his jaw.

After covering Guest with a blanket, Madog said, "I fear for you, Mollie."

"You know I must do it." I hugged my knees close to my chest and waited for Aislinn.

With every breath I drew, I told myself I'd rescue Thomas, we'd return to our cottage, and Mam and Dadoe would be happy again. This long, hard journey would end like a fairy tale, with all of us, even Guest, living happily ever after.

13

AISLINN CAME AS QUIETLY as before and knelt beside me. No one but me saw or heard her. Guest slept and Madog dozed. Aidan had gone to make sure the horses were ready to go when needed.

"Put on the cloak," Aislinn whispered.

As soon as I dropped the hood over my head, she took my hand and led me into the forest. "Are you certain the Kinde Folke won't see me?" I whispered.

"Only if you're simple enough to throw the hood back. Keep covered and all will be well."

She pressed a finger to her lips. "No more talking. Remember to wait until Tiarnach grows drowsy before you take him."

As we neared the circle of stones, I heard the same melancholy tune Madog played on his flute. Here in the Dark Lands, it flowed from my ears into my veins and entered my heart, where I knew it would stay.

"The music," I whispered. "It's so beautiful."

"Beware, our music casts a spell on mortals. No matter how much you yearn to, do not join the dancers. If you do, you'll dance with us for a hundred mortal years."

She reached into her cloak and brought out a small vial. "Don't be alarmed. 'Tis beeswax, nothing more." She pressed a ball of wax into each of my ears. "It will help you resist the music."

Immediately, the music faded to a low hum, scarcely louder than a bee in a field of clover. I wanted to rip the wax from my ears, but Aislinn urged me to follow her uphill between massive tree trunks, shoulder-high ferns, and moss-covered boulders.

And then the tall stones were before us, like sentinels guarding the Kinde Folke. In a long line, dancers wove between the stones, twisting and leaping, their bodies so limber as to seem boneless.

Wreathed with garlands and ribbons, the women's long hair floated around them, rising and falling with every movement. Their silken gowns swirled as weightless as gossamer. Jewels glittered on their bodices and hems.

Although their hair was not as long, the men wore garlands too. They were clad in tunics of dark rich colors, embroidered with moons and stars and symbols whose meanings I didn't know.

So graceful they were, so lithe. Even without hearing the music, I longed to join the dance.

Aislinn pinched my arm so hard, I winced and jerked away from her.

"Remember why you're here," she whispered. "If you join the dance, I will be in peril. And so will you and your precious brother."

She pointed to a slab in the center of the circle. "There is the high table. Your brother sits near the queen. The vacant chair between them is mine. Wait here and watch. I'll signal when it is time to act. As I said, be quick, be silent, and stay covered."

I watched her circle the dancers and seat herself between the queen and Thomas at the high table. My brother wore a scarlet velvet suit, its jacket bejeweled with sparkling stones and embroidered with gold thread. His face was beautiful but as haughty as if he were Kinde Folke born and bred. He frowned at Aislinn and whispered something to her. She patted his hand. For the first time since I'd come to the Dark Lands, I saw him smile.

All around me, the dancers leapt and spun. They neither smiled nor laughed as they kept the music's rhythm. From the shadows, children watched. Some practiced leaping and spinning; others swayed in time to the music, but their faces were solemn. Many of them had a sickly look, pale, thin, and delicate in face and body. They needed sunshine, I thought, and a dose of Mam's spring tonic.

The child closest to me looked in my direction, his face worried. I was sure he couldn't see me, but I scarcely dared to breathe for fear of giving myself away.

The girl beside him touched his arm. "Kaelyn, what do you see in the shadows?"

Kaelyn frowned. "I see nothing, but yet . . ." He shivered and moved closer to her. "Sebilla, do you not feel a presence?"

Sebilla leaned around him. Her face nearly touched my cloak. "I sense nothing, but I do not share your gift." She took his hand. "Come, this is a cold spot. Let us move closer to the fire."

Trembling, I watched the two walk away. Kaelyn continued to look back at the space I occupied, his face filled with doubt. When they at last vanished into the crowd of onlookers, I moved cautiously to a different place. This time, I made sure to keep a good distance between myself and the onlookers.

At the high table, Thomas ate from a golden plate heaped with meat and fish and fruit. I was now as close to the table as I dared to be. The aroma of food filled my nose and made my mouth water. If only I could sit next to my brother and share the feast.

A harper took a place near me and began to play for the diners at the high table. Despite the wax in my ears, I heard him clearly. Caught up in talk and laughter, no one but me paid him any mind, but his music was the most beautiful I'd heard yet. The melody was sad but joyful, slow but fast, loud but soft. The notes seemed to drop over me like a silver net, trapping me in their rhythm.

I drew nearer to the harper, nearer. My feet moved in time to the music as if they had a mind to dance whether I wanted to or not. My hips swayed.

Aislinn saved me by knocking over her glass. It was full to the brim with dark red wine, and as a blood-colored pool spread across the table, Aislinn cried out in dismay.

Startled, I remembered where I was and stepped away

from the harper. Unlike Kaelyn, the harper didn't sense my presence. He paused in his playing to look at the queen.

"Stupid, clumsy girl!" The queen slapped Aislinn's face so hard, the girl nearly fell from her chair.

"Please forgive me, Your Majesty. I am heartily sorry for my clumsiness."

The queen scowled at Aislinn, whose head was bent in repentance. Raising a hand, she snapped her fingers. "Bring more wine," she cried to a servant hovering nearby. "But give none to this one. She's had more than enough already."

As the servant began to pour the wine, my knees felt so weak, I nearly sank to the ground. It was almost time to rescue my brother. I had to succeed. If I failed, we'd both die—Thomas as a sacrifice to the Dark Lord, and myself most likely by the queen's own hand. No matter how she chose to kill me, it would be the worst way possible.

I'd never see Mam and Dadoe again. Or our farm. Or our village. Or the sunlight of the mortal world.

At that moment, I wanted nothing more than to forsake Thomas and flee. Madog, Guest, Aidan, and I would escape from the Dark Lands long before the Wild Hunt began its pursuit.

I looked again at the high table. There sat Thomas looking straight ahead while the servant poured the wine for the queen. Skipping Aislinn, he began to fill the golden goblet in front of Thomas. With a quick movement, Aislinn dropped something into the wine before Thomas picked up the goblet. No one but me saw her do it.

There was no escape for me now. Succeed or fail, live or die, I must do what I'd come to do.

The queen cried out, "Here's to Prince Tiarnach, soon to be wed to Aislinn, daughter of Lady Duatha, and thence to be crowned our king."

The dancers raised their goblets high and shouted, "Hooray for Prince Tiarnach. May his life and his rule be joyous!"

The children threw caps into the air and cried, "Hooray for the prince! Hooray! Hooray!"

Thomas gave the crowd a proud smile and raised his goblet. As he drank, the crowd cheered again, louder this time, their faces flushed from their own wine.

Thomas put down his goblet and sat back in his chair. Aislinn leaned toward him and urged him to finish his wine. Smiling at her, he lifted the goblet and tipped back his head to empty it.

The music began again, louder and faster, and the crowd continued to cheer.

I stood still and watched Thomas. It was clear he enjoyed the applause and the cheering.

Slowly the drink took effect. Thomas's eyes drooped. His head tilted back. Aislinn whispered in his ear. She smiled at him; she stroked his hair; she sang softly.

The queen seemed to have forgotten Thomas. When one of her lords asked her to dance, she laughed and followed him into the crowd. Aislinn signaled to me. It was time.

As quietly as possible I crept to the high table and stood behind my brother.

"He sleeps," Aislinn whispered. "The potion has done as I intended. Take him under your cloak, and leave quickly and quietly."

As I reached for Thomas, she added, "He will sleep for a long time, likely until you are in your own land."

"Thank you for all you've done, Aislinn."

"Good luck to you, Mollie."

Blocking Thomas from the dancers' view, she helped me pull the cloak over Thomas's head. "Do not rest until you are safely out of the Dark Lands."

With my brother hidden under my cloak, I left the stone circle and carried him into the forest. The music slowly faded, and the darkness swallowed up the light from the lanterns.

14

THOMAS WAS HEAVIER THAN I'd expected. My arms ached from the weight of him. I stumbled and staggered on the hillside, slipping on the mossy earth but hurrying on, terrified of hearing the Kinde Folke's laughter turn to curses when they discovered their tithe was gone.

"Mollie, let me help you." Madog appeared from the trees and took Thomas from me. "Hurry, the horses are waiting on the path."

From behind came a cry, and then another and yet another. I ran faster, the hood from my cloak falling back, but all that mattered now was staying as close as possible to Madog and Thomas.

When we finally broke out of the forest, I saw Aidan sitting on a dappled stallion. Beside him, looking pitifully small and helpless, Guest perched atop a dark mare. Madog vaulted to the back of the biggest one of all, a black stallion almost a match for the Pooka, and set Thomas in front of himself. I mounted the mare in front of Guest, and he wrapped his arms around me.

Glad for the times Dadoe had let me ride his big plow horse, I dug my heels into the mare's sides and off we went.

Leading the way, Madog galloped ahead. Although the night was dark and the air dense with fog and mist, the horses neither faltered nor stumbled but almost flew through the dripping trees.

Madog heard the Kinde Folke first. "They're coming!" At his urging, our horses ran even faster.

And, yes, I soon heard them too. A pounding of hooves in the distance. Shouts and cries of rage, the yelping of hounds. It was the Wild Hunt led by the queen. I pictured her face, hard as snow in winter. She would show us no mercy.

Guest whimpered. His arms held me tightly, his head pressed against my back. He was scared, but I had no time to comfort him.

Aiden cursed. "Is this what you wanted?" he shouted at Madog. "To be captured and tortured and killed like dogs? And all for a changeling and a mortal girl."

Madog ignored him and urged the stallion to run faster.

Behind us, the Kinde Folke drew nearer. Their hounds bayed.

Our horses galloped so fast, the forest was a dark blur of trees, a tunnel in which we were trapped. Aidan was right to blame me. Had I watched my tongue in the garden, had I not taken the locket, Thomas and I would be safe with Mam and Dadoe instead of riding to our deaths in the Dark Lands. But where would Guest be?

The hounds were upon us, dark, long and lean, red-eyed and sharp-toothed, more like shadows than actual dogs. They nipped at the horses' legs, leapt at their throats, and tried to pull us to the ground.

And then the queen arrived. She silenced the hounds. They crouched at her feet, tense with a longing to tear us to pieces. At any moment, one of them would sink his teeth into my leg and drag me from my horse. Guest would fall with me. My stomach clenched with fear.

Madog turned his horse to face the queen. Thomas slept in his arms, his head lolling to the side. Aidan and I flanked Madog. It terrified me to be this close to the queen. I kept a brave face, but my heart beat so loudly, she must have heard it. Behind me, Guest shook so hard, my own body trembled.

"Give me the boy," the queen commanded. "And I'll let the rest of you go. He's what I want. You mean nothing to me or mine."

Madog held my sleeping brother tighter. "I cannot do that. I've given my word to take him to his true parents."

"Giving your word to mortals means nothing. *They* mean nothing."

"That may be true for you and your kind, but for me and my kind, it means much."

"Speak for yourself, Madog," Aidan snarled. "Give her the boy. What do you care what they do with him?"

"I have made an oath to Cernunnos," the queen said. "An oath that cannot be broken. When he comes tomorrow, he expects to receive his tithe. If he does not, he will scatter us like dead leaves. Do you wish to see the end of us?"

Madog stared into the queen's eyes. "Truly, I care not a whit what happens to you and yours. You are a cruel and deceptive people. I hope the Dark Lord does indeed scatter you like dead leaves across the land."

The queen stood up in her stirrups. Her warriors raised their spears, and the hounds bared their teeth.

"Madog, you are a fool." Aidan reached for Thomas, but Madog tightened his grip. "Give him to her!"

Whip in hand, the queen came closer. "The boy must be sacrificed. We have no other mortal to use in his place."

As she raised her whip to strike Madog, he grabbed it from her. At the same moment, his horse reared and the queen fell to the ground. Unhurt, she sprang to her feet, her face twisted with rage.

"How dare you, Madog! I will have all of you killed, starting with the girl!"

All the beauty was gone from her. Her face had the hardness of bone, and her eyes had shrunk deeply into their sockets. Her fingers were as sharp-clawed as a hawk's talons.

Turning to me, Madog thrust a heavy pouch into my hands. "Open it and throw the contents at them. Be quick."

I fumbled with the cord and then hurled the sack at the Kinde Folke. Its contents exploded in a flash of lightning. Small iron balls shot into the Kinde Folke crowded around us. They screamed in pain and tried to shield themselves. Horses rose on their hind legs, and their riders fell from their backs. Many lay still on the ground. Others turned their horses and galloped back the way they'd come. Riderless horses followed them. The hounds scattered, howling in agony.

Untouched by the iron balls, the queen mounted her horse.

"Curses on you, Madog," she screamed. "May you die the death of the miserable cur you are!"

Still shouting, she rode after her warriors.

"Go!" Madog cried to Aidan and me. "Go!"

Our three horses ran through the forest, leaping streams, striking sparks from stone, traveling with a speed no mortal horse could match. It was as if I rode the Pooka's back again. At any moment, I expected to soar above the trees.

When we'd put a great distance between us and the queen, Madog slowed the horses to a walk.

"Is it safe to go so slowly?" I asked. The baying of the hounds still rang in my ears, and I couldn't believe we'd truly left them behind. Or the queen. Her angry face hung in my memory like a death mask.

"The queen's huntsmen are in pain from the iron. They're not fit to pursue us." He smiled. "Even the Kinde Folke have their weaknesses."

"It's lucky you got such noble horses for us," I said. "Wherever did you find them?"

He winked. "That's not for you to know."

"Tell the truth, Madog. You stole them from the Kinde Folke. You must have. No mortal horses can run as fast as these."

"They are indeed a rare breed." He patted the stallion's neck. "And that's all I have to say on the matter."

"What about the sack of iron balls?" I asked. "How did you come upon that?"

"You ask too many questions, Mollie-o. I'm certain you know the fate of curious cats." He smiled. "And remember, unlike them, you have only one life, not nine."

Thomas moaned and lay back against Madog's chest. His face was pale, his closed eyes heavy with sleep. Thinking he had a bad dream, I leaned toward him to smooth his tangled curls.

Madog stopped me. "Don't wake him. Perhaps sleep will restore him to the boy he once was."

"But what if the boy he once was is gone forever?"

"It may take time. He's been with the Kinde Folke nearly all his life. You must be patient, Mollie."

We rode on in silence. From the soft warmth of his body, I knew Guest slept as deeply as Thomas. I'd never been so weary in my life, but I was too worried to let myself sleep.

I glanced at Aidan, who rode alone, looking straight ahead, his face no happier than usual.

"I'm so glad to be safe from the queen," I said. "Aren't you?"

Aidan glanced at me. "We won't be safe until the Dark

Lord destroys their power and makes them mortal like us. They'll have no home. They'll be beggars and thieves, hated wherever they go."

"But what of Aislinn and Duatha? Will that be their fate?"

Aidan turned his face away. "I know not. Nor do I care. Lady Duatha should not have lain with Madog."

"You have a hard heart, Aidan."

"At least I'm not stupid."

"I'd rather be stupid than heartless."

"Well, then, you have your wish, don't you?" With that, he tapped the horse's sides with his heels and rode away.

Behind me, Guest stirred restlessly, half-awake, but Thomas slept on. Madog hummed softly and guided the stallion gently so as not to wake him.

No one spoke to me. And I spoke to no one. It was a long, silent ride.

15

THAT EVENING WE PASSED the signpost pointing to Port Riverton. We were out of the Dark Lands at last. As night fell, we made camp in Mirkwood.

Madog laid Thomas on the ground and covered him with a blanket. My brother didn't open his eyes and slept as if he never meant to wake up. Aislinn must have poured a powerful potion into his wine.

Aidan built a fire, and we gathered around it to share a meal of apples, bread, and cheese. I put a portion aside for Thomas in case he awoke, but he lay motionless under his blanket.

As soon as I'd eaten, I bedded down next to Thomas, and Guest snuggled beside me. As usual, he fell asleep at once, and I lay awake listening to the night sounds. Every twig that snapped, every leaf that rustled frightened me. We weren't very far from the Dark Lands. What was to stop the queen from sending her men after us?

I reached for my cloak, thinking I'd sleep better if I was invisible. Although I was sure I'd clasped it around my throat, the cloak was gone. I sat up and began searching for it.

"What are you looking for?" Madog asked.

"The cloak Aislinn gave me. Have you seen it?"

"Surely you didn't believe you'd be allowed to take a cloak of invisibility home with you? Imagine the mischief you'd cause."

"I was cold," I fibbed, "and the cloak would have kept me warm."

"You have the same blanket you've always had and a fire to keep you warm. Go to sleep now, and let me rest."

Long before dawn, quarreling voices awoke me. Aidan and Madog sat a few feet away, their backs to me.

Suddenly Aidan jumped to his feet. "I cannot abide this foolishness another moment," he said. "I want no more of the girl and her brother and the changeling. Stay with them if you wish, but I'm going home."

"Aidan, will you be a fool all your life? Guest is my son, and Mollie has proved to be a brave girl and a wise one, far wiser than you. I must see them home, a day's journey from here. Stay with us. You and I—"

"You and I are nothing," Aidan said. "I came here for one thing. To beg you to return to my mother, who is your wife. If you will not do that, I have no use for you."

"Go, then. But I'm sorely disappointed in you. A jealous child is what you are."

"If you wish to see me again, come home to my mother and me."

With that, he mounted his horse and rode off into the forest. Madog watched him, head cocked as he listened to the horse's hooves long after he lost sight of his son. With a sigh, he sat down by the fire's embers, his head bowed.

Even though I wanted to go to him, I lay still. I'd witnessed something I wasn't meant to see. It was best to leave Madog with his thoughts for now.

Closing my eyes, I slipped back into sleep.

The next time I opened them, morning had come. Madog was roasting potatoes over the fire, and Guest squatted beside him. Thomas slept, curled into a ball with his back to me.

"Thomas?" I leaned over him to make sure he was breathing.

His eyes opened a crack and closed again. Shifting his position, he sighed and slept again.

I tuned to Madog. "Thomas should eat something."

"Let him sleep until we leave Mirkwood. He can eat then."

After we'd had our fill, Madog lifted Thomas onto the stallion, climbed up behind him, and signaled me to follow with Guest.

We hadn't ridden far when a strange darkness fell upon us, turning Mirkwood as black as night. Thunder crashed so loudly the earth seemed to shake. Lightning exploded across the sky with a force that split clouds. The wind rose in a gale so strong that the woods' ancient trees bent before it. The air filled with leaves, and limbs of enormous size broke and crashed to the ground around us.

This was no ordinary storm. Terrified by its force, I crouched low on the mare's back. Guest tightened his grip on me until I feared my ribs would snap. The horses stamped and whinnied, and their manes blew in the wind like unraveling strands of rope.

Then, as quickly as it came, the storm ended, leaving behind a dreadful stillness.

From somewhere, perhaps the sky itself, a mighty voice roared, "You broke your vow to me. Begone!" Tiny cries answered, their words lost in the distance. The voice shouted with rage, "Live in misery and die in pain! You are lost to me and I to you!"

The wind returned in wild gusts, carrying with it a horde of dry leaves. They flew past us and scattered in all directions.

I didn't raise my head from the horse's neck until the wind died. Then I looked at Madog. His head down, he hunched on the stallion's back, and Thomas slept undisturbed in his arms.

With Guest clinging to me, I nudged the mare closer to Madog's horse. "Was that him?" I whispered. "The Dark Lord?"

Madog patted my shoulder comfortingly. "I believe he's destroyed the Kinde Folke just as I said he would."

I remembered the leaves flying past me in the storm and the cries I'd heard. "Are we safe from them now?"

"Nothing about the Kinde Folke is ever certain. Even though they're now scattered across the world, those ones will search for other tribes and seek to join them."

"But those other tribes are far from here, are they not?"

"The Folke are wanderers just as travelers are. They never stay in one place long. Who's to say whether they're far or near?"

He looked at me and guessed my fear. "Don't worry, Mollie. They'll be too busy learning to live as mortals to hunt for you or your brother."

"But suppose the queen regains her power? She might—"

"She won't. She can't. Her power and her magic are gone."

"But are you sure?"

"As sure as I can be, Mollie. Stop your fretting, and keep your thoughts on Thomas and how to wash the Kinde Folke from his memory. And from your memory as well."

"But what of Duatha and Aislinn? Where will they go? What will become of them?"

Madog lowered his head and hid his face from me. "I know not, Mollie. Don't ask again."

I said no more about Duatha, for it was clear it gave Madog pain to speak of her. In silence, I pondered their fate, as well as that of the children I'd seen. Duatha and Aislinn were strong, but what of Kaelyn and Sebilla? They were little and helpless. How would they fare begging on the roads?

Slowly Mirkwood became sunnier. Birds called overhead. I tilted my head back to search for them among the leaves. Mockingbirds, robins, thrushes, larks—the first I'd seen for a long while. Gradually the trees grew farther apart, and more light poured down through their leaves. Shadows lost their menace, and I glimpsed patches of blue sky.

At first, my mood brightened with the day, but as we came closer to the end of Mirkwood, I lowered my head and watched the mare's dainty hooves. Every step took me nearer to home. Although I longed to feel Mam's arms around me and smell Dadoe's pipe smoke, I was worried about Thomas.

He still slept, his head bumping gently against Madog's chest. His eyelids twitched, and his hand brushed at his face as if the sunlight bothered him.

What would he say when he woke up?

16

IN THE AFTERNOON, WE came to the top of a hill overlooking Lower Hexham and the farms surrounding it. In the distance, I spied our cottage. Mam was hanging out the wash, and Dadoe was working in the garden. From where I stood, they were no bigger than my thumb.

Guest leaned around me. "Do you see your house?"

I pointed. "It's there, where Mam is hanging clothes on the line. See?"

"I see her, I see her. And the man—is he Dadoe?"

"Yes, that's Dadoe."

I turned to Madog. "Are you coming with us?"

"I think not, Mollie," he said. "It's best for you three to go alone."

"But what if they welcome Thomas and me, but not Guest?"

"Should things go badly, I'll be near. I give you my word."

With Thomas still dozing in his arms, Madog slid off his

horse. Speaking softly, he told me to dismount and help Guest down. Gently he set Thomas on my horse and fashioned a bridle from his belt. Looping makeshift reins around Thomas, he did his best to secure him on the mare's back.

Then Madog whispered into the mare's ear. She nodded her head as if she understood.

"Now, my lad, it's time to say goodbye." Madog lifted Guest above his head and laughed. "Look, you—this is how far you'll see when you're a man. Between now and then, I mean to visit you often and watch you grow and prosper."

Turning to me, Madog bowed.

"Farewell and good luck, Mollie," he said. "You'll see me again before long, but until then, it's been a pleasure and an honor to know you, stubborn though you are."

"But what of this horse? How am I to return her to you?"

"Don't you worry. As soon as Thomas puts his feet on the ground, the horse will return to me."

Tipping his hat, he leapt on the stallion and rode back toward Mirkwood.

With sorrow, I watched him ride away. *A man you don't meet every day*, he'd once said of himself. And I knew it was true. I'd never see Madog's like again, I was certain.

With the mare following close behind, Guest and I walked down the path and across the fields. I had no wish to pass through the village. Men, women, and children would stop us on every street to ask about Thomas and stare at Guest.

Grasshoppers leapt out of our way, and a raven watched us from a fence post. Guest chased the grasshoppers but never managed to catch one. Thomas slept on the mare's back.

"We're almost home," I told Guest. "Do you remember anything?"

Guest hopped from one foot to another and laughed. "I was little-bitty babby then. I doesn't remember nothing, except I were bad—bite, scratch. I were nasty. Mam was hating me, Mollie, too. I were lonesome, I were scared, my belly were aching."

He laughed again and clapped his hands. "I are not bad now like then, Mollie. True? No more biting, no more scratching, no more hitting, no more kicking. I talks now. I walks. I chews food with my teeth. Mam and Dadoe will see me changed so much. They will lets me stay."

Guest's words tumbled out so fast, I had trouble keeping up with what he was saying. Crossing my fingers behind my back and hoping it was true, I said, "Mam and Dadoe will love you like I do. Just wait and see."

"Good." Waving his skinny arms and almost tripping over his own feet, Guest chased a butterfly in circles.

Behind us, Thomas muttered something. I went to the mare's side and peered up at him. His eyes opened slowly, and he stared about in confusion.

"Don't worry, Thomas. You're safe now. The queen is far away. She cannot take you again." I spoke soothingly, thinking to comfort him, but he stared down at me with anger.

"You! It's you, isn't it? You've taken me from my people and brought me to your land! You must return me at once."

"No, Thomas, you don't understand. I've saved your life." In a rush of words, I told him the truth. "The Kinde Folke never meant for you to be their king. You were to be their tithe to the Dark Lord."

"Liar! Take me back to the Dark Lands. I demand it. You cannot keep me here."

"Thomas, please, this is your home. Our cottage is under that tree. Soon Mam and Dadoe will see us and come running."

In anger, Thomas jumped off the mare. As soon as his feet

touched the ground, the mare turned and galloped back the way we'd come. At the same moment, Thomas's fine velvet suit turned to tattered leaves. The gems on his jacket became acorns, and the gold trim became moss. All that remained of his fine leather boots was mud caking his legs and feet. Instead of a sword, a crooked stick hung by his side.

Thomas stared at himself in dismay. "What have you done with my suit and my boots?" He raised the stick as if it were a sword, saw what it was, and threw it to the ground. "You've stolen everything from me, even my sword."

"I stole nothing from you, Thomas. Your fancy clothes were always what you see now — leaves, sticks, acorns, mud, and moss. You've been sorely cheated by the Kinde Folke. Not by me."

"I was their prince," he insisted. "They loved me, I tell you. They *loved* me. They gave me everything I asked for. They did whatever I told them to do."

"Thomas, you must believe me. You're my brother. I love you. Mam and Dadoe love you. Don't make them unhappy. They've longed for you to come home."

But Thomas refused to listen. "My name is Tiarnach. You are not my sister. The peasants who live in that hovel are not my mother and father. They mean nothing to me. Less than nothing. I will never love them or you or anyone—especially not the toad."

Thomas turned his angry eyes on Guest, who had crept close to me. Raising his fist, he aimed a blow at the changeling, but I grabbed his arm to stop him.

"You will not hurt Guest. Not now. Not ever."

Thomas stared at me in confusion. "Why did you bring me here? The light is so bright, it hurts my eyes. There's so much noise, I cannot hear myself speak. I hate you and everyone else in this miserable place!"

He turned and began running across the field toward Mirkwood, now a distant line of trees on the horizon. I ran after him and caught him. Thomas lacked the strength to fight, so I pulled him step by step toward the cottage. With every move he made, more of his clothing disintegrated. He looked like a small tree shedding leaves.

With a worried face, Guest watched Thomas and me struggle. "Thomas is the changeling now," he said. "Kick, bite, hit, scream, and cry."

"How dare you?" Thomas tried to break away from me, but I had a good tight grip on his arm.

We finally reached the garden gate. From the kitchen came the smell of fresh-baked bread.

Thomas stared past me at the cottage. "The Kinde Folke wouldn't keep pigs in a hovel like this."

Too angry to answer, I pushed open the gate. The daisies by the door were in bloom, and a morning glory vine climbed the walls, filling the air with sweetness.

As timid as if I'd come to a stranger's house, I knocked softly.

Inside, Dadoe said, "Someone's here, Agnes."

Mam's light footsteps crossed the floor. I held my breath and clutched Thomas's hand so tightly, he yelped. Guest ducked behind me.

The door opened and there stood Mam, plumper now that she no longer nursed Guest night and day. Her eyes widened at the sight of me.

"Sam!" she cried. "Mollie's come home! She's here, on the doorstep."

Throwing her arms around me, she held me tightly. "We never thought to see you again. Where have you been all this time? Surely you never went to the Dark Lands?"

Dadoe lifted me right off my feet. "Mollie, Mollie, my dear Mollie. Oh, how we've missed you!"

Gazing into his happy face, I hugged him tight. He'd be even happier to see Thomas.

When Dadoe put me down, he saw Thomas. "Who is this boy? And why, in the name of all that's holy, is he dressed in leaves?"

Thomas drew himself up as if his tattered coat of leaves were a velvet jacket trimmed with gems and gold. "I am Prince Tiarnach," he said. "And I demand to be returned to my people. This dirty ragged peasant has brought me here against my will."

I tugged at Dadoe's hand to get his attention. "Don't believe him, Dadoe, it's Thomas, your son—I've brought him home. Surely you know him. You must!"

Dadoe turned to me, his face angry. "Have you lost your wits, Mollie? Thomas is a baby. This boy is at least seven years old."

In desperation, I tugged at Mam's skirt. "Please, please, tell me you know your own son when you see him. You must!"

Mam lowered her head. "Why have you brought him here? Who is he? Where is he from? He's not Thomas. He can't be."

"Mollie must be under a spell," Dadoe mumbled. "Why else would she behave this way?"

"Look again, both of you," I begged. "I swear on my life that boy is Thomas. He's older because time goes different in the Dark Lands."

Mam studied Thomas. He stood as before, head up, perhaps too proud to speak to us.

"His hair's the right color," Mam said slowly. "And his eyes are the same shade of blue."

Dadoe stepped closer and peered at Thomas. "He looks like our son might at this age," he said grudgingly, "but someone has tricked you, Mollie."

"Thomas was a happy baby," Mam said, "but this boy has no sparkle in his eye, no joy in his heart."

With scorn in his voice, Thomas finally spoke. "Indeed, you speak the truth. I am not Thomas. I am Tiarnach, prince of the Kinde Folke and destined to be their king."

Mam turned to me in horror. "You've stolen a Kinde One? Oh, Mollie, they'll come for him with a vengeance. We'll be destroyed."

"You must take him back and beg their forgiveness," Dadoe said. "Remember what they did to the Millers' barn and house—burned them both to the ground just because Mistress Miller refused to call them kind."

I struggled to hold back my tears. "You don't know the danger I've faced to bring this ungrateful boy home. I've been to the Dark Lands and back. I've fought the Kinde Folke and faced their queen. I've seen the destruction of the Kinde Folke at the hands of Cernunnos. And yet you refuse to believe that this is *Thomas,* your son, standing in front of you."

Granny Hedgepath pushed open the gate and hobbled to us. "Let me see, let me see."

At the sight of her, Thomas stepped back. He looked like a frightened boy, not a proud prince. "Keep away," he cried. "You're a witch—I smell earth magic on you."

"And I smell Kinde Folke magic on you, but I also smell your mortal flesh and bones."

Granny turned to me. "I never thought you'd do it, girl, but you brung your brother home. Now all you got to do is tame him."

Dadoe stared at Granny in amazement. "What wild tale is this?"

"It ain't a wild tale, Master Cloverall. The girl is telling the truth. That's your boy Thomas, grown older in the Dark Lands."

"Then why doesn't he know his own name? Why doesn't he remember us?"

Mam looked at Dadoe. "Tell me, Sam, do you remember the first months of your life? Do I? Does Mollie? Of course not. No one does."

Granny nodded. "He was a baby when he was took. All he knows is his life with the Kinde Folke. Like I said, you got to tame him."

Granny tilted her head like a crow and looked Thomas over. "You might want to start with them leaves he's wearing. Wash him and get him into decent clothing."

"No one tames me." Thomas seemed to have gotten over his fear of Granny now. "I know who I am and where I belong."

"I wish you good luck with that one, Sam." Granny laughed. "I wager you'll find the other one a sight easier to deal with."

"What other one?" Dadoe called, but Granny was already out of the gate and hurrying away.

"She must have meant Mollie," Mam said. "She's a biddable girl."

Thomas snickered. "Just wait until you see what else Mollie has brought you."

Mam and Dadoe didn't hear what he said, but I did. I looked around for Guest, but he seemed to have vanished.

Before I had a chance to go in search of him, Mam took my hands in hers and looked into my eyes. "Since both you and Granny say this boy is Thomas, I will treat him as if he *is* Thomas, even though in my heart I cannot believe it." She looked at Dadoe. "Will you do the same, Sam?"

He sighed. "Give me time to smoke my pipe in the garden. There's much to ponder before I make up my mind."

"Help me get the boy into the house. He and Mollie must be both hungry and thirsty."

While Dadoe struggled to get Thomas inside, I went in search of Guest.

I finally spied him in the lane talking to the peddler. A fine new horse, much too good for the job, pulled the cart. Tall and glossy black he was, with a long mane and tail.

When Guest saw me, he waved and I ran to the cart.

"Well, well," the peddler said. "Whose boy is this, Miss Mollie Cloverall? I've not seen him here before."

"Oh yes you have, but Guest was a baby then. Now he's grown big and strong."

"Surely you're not telling me this is the babby you were

carrying that night I met you on the bridge? The one you were taking to the travelers?"

"It's the very same one. I kept him after all. Isn't he grand now?"

The peddler laughed. "Yes, indeed he is, and so are you, Mollie. You've grown some yourself since that night."

Something about the peddler's laugh was familiar. And his teeth—they were so much younger than his wrinkled face.

Guest moved closer to the peddler and sniffed and sniffed again. His eyes opened wide, and he looked at me. We both knew who the peddler was now.

"It seems you got yourself a new horse," I said, "and a fine one at that. What happened to the sorry broken-down horse you had the last time you visited?"

"I made a good trade at the horse fair." He grinned like a sly fox. "I'm a man who knows how to bargain."

Guest hopped around him and laughed. "I knows that horse. I seen him before!"

"All black horses look the same," the peddler said.

"This one has the look of a Kinde Folke horse," I said. "And you have the eyes of a man I know, the sort you don't meet every day."

"Oh my, there's no fooling the two of you." Madog spread his hands, palms out, and laughed. "You are indeed a clever pair."

Guest tugged at Madog's white bushy beard.

"Ouch," Madog cried. "Leave it be."

"Is it real?" I asked.

"For now it is." He rubbed his face. "Disguises are a gift we travelers have. It comes in handy when a trade goes bad or we're caught in a lie."

"How do you do it?" I asked.

"We turn our backs, and when we turn around, you see a different person."

"Be Madog," Guest begged.

The peddler hopped down from his cart and turned his back. When he turned around, there was Madog, young and straight and full of merriment.

He turned again and there was the peddler. "It's a good disguise for a man in this tricky world of yours. No one pays any mind to an old man roaming the roads with goods to sell."

"Perhaps you should disguise your horse as well," I said.

"Yes. Perhaps I should. This one is bound to draw many an envious eye."

"Now," he said, "before I leave, I have gifts for you."

To Guest he gave a tin flute like the one he himself played.

"This like yours," Guest said. "You makes pretty music. I makes pretty music." He blew into the flute and managed to make a few shrill tweets. "It not work good."

"You must learn to play it, Guest," Madog said. "Keep the flute and try and try. After a while, you'll play a nice tune."

Holding the flute tightly in one fist, Guest said, "I see pretty ribbons. Mollie likes ribbons."

"Does she now?" Madog reached into a sack and pulled out a handful of bright-colored ribbons. "Do any of these suit you?"

I studied the colors streaming from his hand—pinks, yellows, blues, purples, reds, and every color in between—a rainbow of ribbons. I fingered them, holding up one and then another. "I'll have the red, if you please."

"You may have all of them, Mollie my dear, for you've earned them and much more." With one deft flourish, he draped dozens of ribbons around my neck, stood back, and smiled.

"Pretty, pretty, pretty." Guest blew into his flute and out

came another squawk. He laughed. "I try hard, I make pretty music for Mollie."

Madog climbed onto his seat and picked up the horse's reins. "I must go now. Be good, be careful, and if Guest is not treated well, you'll hear from me."

"Stay," Guest cried.

"That I cannot do. I have matters to tend to. My other son for one, my wife for another."

"But when will you be back?" I asked.

"When the wind blows me this way, I reckon."

"That's no answer."

"Truthfully, Mollie, I cannot name a day or even a month, but I promise you'll see me again." He turned to Guest. "Be a good boy-o. Play me a tune when I return."

"Don't go. Stay, Madog, stay here." Tears ran down Guest's dirty face.

"I'll miss you, Guest." He winked at me. "I'll miss Mollie, too. It's a long and perilous journey we three have shared."

He leaned down to give me a swift kiss on the cheek. "Be brave, Mollie. Be smart. You're a fine lass," he said to me.

"Walk on," he told the horse.

Guest and I ran alongside the cart, but our legs tired and

we fell behind. Madog waved to us all the way to the top of Cat Tail Hill, but, all too soon, he disappeared down the other side.

I wiped Guest's tears away with the hem of my dress and rubbed my own with my fists. It was time for Guest to meet Mam and Dadoe.

Mam called to me from the cottage door. "Come inside, Mollie. There's a tub of hot water waiting for you."

Guest looked at me in alarm. "Hot water? Will her cook you?"

I laughed. "No, you silly goose. She's going to give me a bath."

"What's a bath?"

"See all this dirt?" I stretched out my arm. I lifted my foot. "A bath will clean it off."

"Will it hurt?"

"No, of course not." I took his hand and led him inside.

Mam had set the big tin tub by the fire and filled it with water. When she saw Guest, she dropped the soap and stared at him in shock. "I thought you left him in the Dark Lands."

Behind her, on the bench by the fire, Thomas ignored us.

While we'd been outside with Madog, he'd had a bath. Mam had dressed him in one of Dadoe's shirts, which hung below his knees. He looked miserable.

Hearing the dismay in Mam's voice, Guest hid behind me.

"I couldn't leave him there, Mam, not with them. They would have let him die. Surely you wouldn't want him to suffer."

I tried to pull him out from behind me so Mam could see him, but Guest refused to budge.

"I can't have him here. The crying, the biting—I can't do it again."

"He's changed, Mam. He doesn't cry or bite now. Indeed, I never would have survived the Dark Lands if he hadn't been with me."

"Your father will never let him stay. He still hasn't made up his mind about Thomas."

With a huge effort, I pulled Guest in front of me. "Look at him, Mam. He walks now. He talks, too. He's learned so much. Please give him a chance."

"I sorry, Mistress Mam," Guest said. "I was bad then, but not now. No more crying and biting and hitting. I be good. I promise."

Mam's face softened. She looked at Guest. She looked at

me. She sighed and shook her head. "Dadoe won't like it, Mollie, you know that."

"What won't Dadoe like?" And there he was, coming through the door, pipe in hand. He hadn't seen Guest yet, but he soon would.

Guest shut his eyes and put his fingers in his ears.

"What is he doing here?" Dadoe stared at Guest. "First you bring home False Thomas and now the changeling? What else have you brought with you?"

"Nothing else, Dadoe, just Guest. Please let him stay. He'll be no trouble, I promise you."

"You're asking me to keep a changeling in my house?" Dadoe's face reddened with anger. "Have you taken leave of your wits?"

Guest clung to my skirt, his head down, as if he feared to look at Dadoe.

Mam spoke up. "I think we have no choice, Sam. We must keep them both. They have nowhere else to go. Would you have them starve by the roadside somewhere?"

Timidly Guest touched Dadoe's trouser leg. "I don't cry and fuss no more, Master Dadoe. I'm a good one now, I am. I help you do things. I work for you."

"You don't have to keep us both," Thomas said. "Send me back to the Kinde Folke, and let the changeling stay."

Dadoe coughed once or twice. He fidgeted with a loose button on his shirt and succeeded in breaking the thread. The sound of the button falling to the floor was unnaturally loud.

"Well, now," Dadoe finally said. "Much as I dislike the idea, much as I'm sure it will come to no good, I'll abide the changeling's presence so long as you keep him out of my way. I don't want him under my feet, tripping me. As for the boy, maybe he'll learn to keep a civil tongue in his head."

"Good enough," Mam said.

I flung my arms around Dadoe. "You won't be sorry, I promise."

Guest clapped his hands and grinned. "I not trip Dadoe. I stay out of the way. Good, I be so good, gooder than anyone."

Thomas said nothing.

"Now," Mam said, "it's bath time for Mollie and Guest."

Guest looked at the tub fearfully. "Will it hurt?"

"I'll go first," I told him. "And you'll see it doesn't hurt."

Mam held up a towel like a curtain, and I stripped off the

dirty rags I'd worn since I'd left home. *Into the fire with them,* I thought.

Once I was in the tub, Mam scrubbed and scoured till my skin turned red. She washed my hair and fretted over the tangles. "It's like a hedge full of thistles and nettles. I'll never get a comb through it."

Wrapped in a towel, I grinned at Guest, who was cowering in a corner. "See? It didn't hurt."

"You said ouch, ouch, ouch," he told me. "I heared you!"

As Mam grabbed him, I climbed the ladder to the loft and opened my chest of clothing. I pulled out clean underwear and a faded flowered dress.

As I struggled to comb my hair, I heard Mam ask Guest, "Have you never had a bath?"

"No. No bath!" Guest wailed. "Soap hurt!"

By the time I came downstairs, Guest looked less like a wild thing and more like a boy. His hair was the color of silver, and his skin was pale. Of course, his ears were still big, his eyes still yellowish, his arms and legs still long and skinny, but maybe people would get used to him and forget who'd left him at our cottage.

Mam had cut a shirt down for Guest. It fit more like a

dress than a shirt, but Guest said, "Look, Mollie. I has shirt." Stretching out his arms, he admired the striped sleeves. "I like. Smells good, feels nice."

Mam smiled. "It's much too big, but at least you're clean and decently clothed for now. I'll make better outfits for you and Thomas when I find time to sit and sew."

She glanced at Thomas, who had fallen asleep on the bench. Touching his curls, she said, "When he's sleeping, he looks more like the baby I remember." She smiled. "Maybe as time passes, he'll come back to us in spirit as well as body and be content."

I hoped so, for it seemed that Thomas's return had brought Mam more sorrow than joy.

"Come now, Thomas," Mam said. "Wake up. It will soon be suppertime. You must be hungry."

He opened his eyes and looked around as if he'd forgotten where he was.

"You're home, Thomas," Mam said softly.

"No," he said. "This isn't my home. And it never will be."

Spying Guest on the other side of the room, he said, "Don't come near me, toad, or I'll smite you."

Guest looked at me. *"Smite?"*

"It means he'll hit you."

"Oh." Guest put more distance between himself and Thomas. "Maybe I smite him."

Mam frowned. "There will be no smiting in this house, Thomas."

"How often must I tell you? My name is Tiarnach, not Thomas. Until you call me by my proper name, I will not speak to you." With that, Thomas crossed his arms over his chest, pressed his lips together in a frown, and stared past us as if we were invisible.

17

OUR FIRST MEAL TOGETHER was not what I'd hoped it would be. Dadoe sat at the head of the table facing Mam, and I took my usual place on the side. Guest sat next to me, and Thomas sat across from me.

Mam heaped our plates with potatoes and carrots and roast chicken. Steam rose, and the aroma made my stomach growl. It had been a long time since I'd eaten a meal served at a table on plates with knives and forks.

Quietly I stopped Guest from eating with his fingers and showed him how to use a knife and fork.

When Thomas saw his plate, he broke his promise not to speak. "If I eat your food, will I be forced to live with you forever?"

"We don't abide by Kinde Folke laws," Mam said.

"How am I to trust you?"

Dadoe shrugged. "We are what we seem. We say what we mean. We don't lie."

Thomas looked doubtful, but he ate one or two mouthfuls of vegetables and looked at the chicken with disgust. "This is peasant food," he muttered. "I cannot eat it."

"Please try a bite of chicken, Thomas," Mam begged. "You must be hungry."

Without answering, he pushed his plate aside and returned to the bench.

Guest gobbled up everything on his plate and asked for more. The rest of us ate silently, chewing and swallowing without really tasting the food. Thomas was a dark presence in the cottage, ruining everything.

When night came, I took Guest up to the loft where I slept. Mam and Dadoe got into their bed and pulled the curtains shut around it. Thomas slept on his bench.

The next day and the next and the ones after that went by in much the same way. Thomas sulked, ate little, and said nothing.

One cool, cloudy morning, we sat in the kitchen enjoying the fire's warmth. Fall had come, and winter would soon follow. Dadoe had left at sunrise to go hunting with other men from the village. He'd promised to be home with a deer before sundown.

Mam was busy knitting wool sweaters for Guest and Thomas. I was darning holes in my stockings, and Guest was playing with the marbles Dadoe had given him. Thomas lay on his bench staring into the fire.

Save for the fire's hiss and murmur, the kitchen was quiet. Perhaps that was why we heard soft voices in the lane near the cottage. Mam went to a window and looked out. "Beggars," she said. "There are more than usual this year."

Giving me a half loaf of bread and a hunk of cheese, she said, "Take this to them. The poor souls look like they're starving."

With Guest behind me, I ran to open the garden gate. Two women stood in the lane. The younger one held the older one's arm as if to help her walk. Although the day was not overly cold, they huddled together, their long cloaks drawn tight against the wind.

When they saw me, they made as if to move on, but I told them they were welcome. "I have food for you. If you wish, you may come inside and eat by the fire."

Guest tugged at my skirt. He shook his head, clearly uneasy.

If he was warning me, he'd waited too long, for the older

woman had already thanked me. "We've traveled a long, hard road. A seat by a fire would be a great comfort."

Hoping to see what Guest saw, I looked into the woman's face, but her hood cast a dark shadow that hid her features.

"Thank you," the young one said. "My mother is weary of travel. We'll rest by the fire a bit and soon be on our way."

I led them inside, but Guest lagged behind the strangers as if he dared not get too close to them. "Don't trust them," he whispered to me. "They smells like smoke and dark."

"You're so silly, Guest. They're beggars, that's all. They travel the roads and cook over fires like we once did." But I, too, noticed something strange about the two—nothing fearsome, just strange.

Mam looked up from her knitting. "Please, come in and take a seat by the fire. I'll make a pot of tea to warm you."

Thomas roused himself from a nap to stare at the women.

Guest lingered in the doorway. I beckoned to him, but he stayed where he was.

The women ate the bread and cheese silently. Their presence made a strangeness in the cottage. Shadows seemed deeper, the air colder, the room less cheerful.

"Well," Mam said in an effort to break the silence. "Where do you come from?"

The woman sighed, and the girl answered in a low voice. "From a distant place to which we can never return."

"I'm sorry to hear that," Mam said. "It must be terrible beyond words to lose your home. So many have been on the road lately."

"Yes," the woman said. "Far more than usual, I think."

Mam refilled their cups with hot tea. "Where are you bound?"

The girl shrugged. "We go where the wind blows us."

Thomas leaned forward, his eyes catching the firelight. "In your travels, have you by chance seen the Kinde Folke?"

Startled to hear him speak, I looked at him.

The girl glanced at him. "What do you know of the Kinde Folke, boy?"

"I'm one of them," he said proudly. "A prince. My name is Tiarnach. Perhaps someone asked about me."

"Tiarnach," the woman repeated. "No, we've not met anyone who asked about you or your whereabouts."

The girl rose from her seat. "You're tired, Mother. Rest by

the fire." Turning to me, she said, "Perhaps you and I might walk in the garden. I feel a need for fresh air."

Outside, the girl looked at me closely. "Do you not remember me, Mollie Cloverall?"

Suddenly fearful, I edged away from her. "Should I?"

Her cloak swirled in the wind. Its fabric had less substance than the shadow of a moth's wing.

She drew back her hood and said, "I am much changed, but surely you've not forgotten me."

Aislinn's face had grown thin. Her eyes were darkly shadowed, her skin as pale as the moon, her thick mass of hair snarled with tangles, but she hadn't lost her beauty.

"Aislinn," I whispered. "What brings you here?"

"Your brother needs our help. Madog believes we can restore Tiarnach to himself."

"Where is Madog? Is he nearby?"

"When we last saw him, he was on his way to the North Kingdom to do business with a tribe of Kinde Folke there."

"Did he say anything about returning to Lower Hexham?"

"Maybe this year in the spring, or next year in the winter. Maybe tomorrow, maybe next month. With Madog, who can say where he'll go, or when? He's a traveler, Mollie, as you well know."

I was not surprised. The ribbons he'd given me would most likely be old and faded when I saw him again.

"Now," Aislinn said, "tell me about Tiarnach. It seems he hasn't yet given up the idea he's a prince."

"Not at all. He's been with us almost three months, but he still hates our ways. He says little but longs to return to the Dark Lands, where he believes he will be king."

"Surely he knows there are no Dark Lands now."

"I've told him many times, but he insists I kidnapped him from the Kinde Folke and stole from him all that is precious. He truly believes you will rescue him from a miserable existence."

"Alas, our existence is far more miserable than his. He's fortunate to be here with you and his true parents."

"If you tell him the truth, perhaps he'll believe it."

Aislinn fidgeted with the ragged edge of her cloak. "Bring him to me. I cannot promise to change him, but I'll talk to him."

In the cottage, Mam and Duatha spoke in low voices.

Thomas sat on his bench and watched them. If he recognized Duatha, he showed no sign of it.

I touched Mam's shoulder. "May I take Thomas outside for a moment?"

"Of course."

Thomas shifted his eyes to me. "Is the other one in the garden?"

"Yes. She has something important to tell you."

"Did she see the Kinde Folke after all? Will she take me to them?" His body trembled with excitement. When he stood up, his legs shook.

For the first time since I'd seen him in the stone circle, I pitied my brother. What he longed for was forever denied him. Somehow he had to content himself with Mam and Dadoe and me.

With Guest close behind, I led Thomas outside. Aislinn rose from the bench and walked toward him.

He stopped a few feet away from her. "Did you see them? Do they seek me?"

"Tiarnach," she said. "Do you not know me?"

When she took his hands in hers, he stepped back, appearing confused and frightened. "What's happened to you? You're not the Aislinn I know—you're pale and weak and older than I thought. You must be an impostor."

Aislinn tightened her grip on his hands and held him firm. "Tiarnach, I am Aislinn, not an impostor. I have come to tell you the truth. You must believe me."

"I will not believe a word you say. You are a liar sent here to deceive me."

Thomas struggled to break away, but Aislinn was stronger than he was.

"Stop fighting me," she said. "The Dark Lands are lost to us. Our palace is in ruins—there's no dancing, no music, no feasting."

"That cannot be true," Thomas wailed.

"I am not a liar," Aislinn insisted, her face fierce with anger. "Why do you think my mother and I are here, dressed in rags, with no home? We are beggars, now, even the queen, doomed to wander the earth, lost and afraid, until we die."

"No, no, no." Thomas began to cry. "I hate you, Aislinn!"

With Mam at her side, Duatha joined us. "You must believe my daughter, Tiarnach. When we lost you, we had no tithe to pay Cernunnos. To punish us, he destroyed all we had, even our magic. We live now as the poorest of mortals. If you return to us, you'll be a beggar, not a king."

"We deceived you," Aislinn said. "We stole you from your parents for one purpose—to give you to Cernunnos as his tithe. To sacrifice you. Everything we told you then was a lie, but we are not lying to you now."

Duatha looked long and hard at Thomas. "We were a cruel people. We did not deserve to be called Kinde. I hope you have not become as heartless as we were."

She took his hand and put it into mine. "Be grateful to your sister. You owe your life to her. Believe me, most who are taken to the Dark Lands are not as fortunate as you."

Thomas's body shook with sobs. "I believed all you told me. I was to marry Aislinn, I was to be king."

Duatha sighed. "We have always put our own kind first, but now that we live as mortals and suffer as you do, our hearts have softened. That's why we're here. We've come to undo the harm done to you."

Aislinn took my brother's hands in hers. "You are *Thomas* now. You must learn to live as mortals live, for you are one of them. It will be hard, but you have Mollie and Guest to help you. You have a mother and father who truly love you and will never let you come to harm."

She released him, but he reached out to her. "Let me come with you. Let me live the life you live, no matter what it is."

Duatha pulled him gently away from Aislinn. "No, Thomas, you must stay here. Your time with us is over."

As Aislinn turned to Mam to say goodbye, Duatha took me aside.

"*Some* of us have learned to be merciful," she said. "Others roam the world seeking revenge. Be vigilant, Mollie. You have enemies among the Kinde Ones even now."

The wind blew colder, and dead leaves rattled down the lane as if they meant to harm us. Guest gripped my hand. A shiver ran through his small body.

Aislinn and Duatha drew their cloaks around themselves and made their way toward Cat Tail Hill. If I hadn't known better, I would have mistaken them for two beggar women.

Mam now stood in the cottage doorway as if she were waiting for Thomas to come to her. With his back turned to all of us, he watched Aislinn and Duatha trudge up Cat Tail Hill.

The way he stood there, all alone, his shoulders hunched against the wind, made me uneasy. If Thomas didn't believe what he'd been told, if he still longed to be with the Kinde Folke, he'd never accept his place in our world.

Weary beyond words, I sank down on the garden bench. Guest sat beside me and reached for my hand. I clasped his tightly, sure now that I'd failed to fix anything by bringing Thomas home. After Aislinn and Duatha disappeared over the top of the hill, Thomas remained by the road, his head bowed in grief. Slowly he turned and looked at Guest and me, almost as if he'd never really seen us before. Without speaking, he walked to the bench and took a seat on my other side.

Cautiously I touched his cold fingers. Instead of yanking his hand away, as I'd expected, he leaned his head against my shoulder and sighed. The three of us sat together in silence.

The wind rose and the trees pelted us with sharp-edged red leaves. Towering gray clouds in the shape of monstrous creatures drifted along the horizon like armies marching to war.

Over our heads, a rook cawed and another answered. One dipped down and brushed my cheek with the tip of its wing. Together the rooks flew toward Mirkwood. Their harsh cries sounded like laughter.

Afterword

Although I've always loved folklore and fairy tales, I doubt I would have written *Guest* if I'd never gone to Ireland.

I took a hiking trip to Ireland a few years ago and spent several days walking in ancient forests of great beauty and mystery—a magical landscape, straight out of fairy tales I'd read as a child. The light was dim and sometimes misty. Moisture hung in the air. My fellow hikers and I found ourselves speaking quietly as if we were afraid to disturb the silence of those ancient woods.

High on a hilltop, we came upon a stone circle, tilted by time but still standing. For over a thousand years the tall stones had stood here, bearing witness to the forgotten people who erected them. Below was a dark lake into which a waterfall cascaded from a cliff. Above was a sky of gray clouds blown to tatters by the wind. No houses in sight, no farms . . . a landscape unchanged since those stones were raised.

In that lonely place, I found the setting for a new book. My story was influenced by the ancient ballad "Tam Lin," which can be found in books of Celtic folklore. Although there are many variants, the story centers on a young woman who rescues a young man held prisoner by the queen of the Sidhe. To save Tam Lin from being tithed to the dark lord, Janet hides in the forest and waits until the queen and her attendants appear. She pulls Tam Lin from his white horse and manages to hold him as he changes shape, assuming the form of savage beasts and poisonous snakes. The defeated queen frees Tam Lin, and he and Janet flee from the forest.

The Sidhe were often called the Kinde Folke, in the hope they would be kind. Although the Sidhe are fairies, they do not live in flowers and fly about on dainty wings. They are a different breed altogether, tall and powerful, feared for their cruelty and trickery. They live underground in glittering palaces located outside of human time and space. Renowned for their bewitching music and dancing, they sometimes lure mortals to join them for a night of festivity. When the mortals awake, they discover they've been gone for a hundred years instead of one night.

Belief in changelings was common in Ireland centuries

ago. It was thought that fairies gave birth to sickly babies, who were often swapped for healthy human babies. When parents discovered that their baby had been replaced by a changeling, their first impulse was to leave it the forest or at a crossroads where it would most likely die. In my story, Agnes Cloverall is persuaded to keep her changeling in the hope that the Kinde Folke will take him back and return her own baby.

The Pooka that Mollie encounters—a beautiful black stallion who dwells in lonely places and is capable of changing his shape—is straight from Irish tales. At times helpful to humans, he can be destructive and dangerous. He appears in many cultures and is believed to be a nature spirit.

Cernunnos is a horned god found in the mythology of the British Isles and Western Europe. Despite his antlers, he is not the devil but a nature spirit like the Pooka. He lives in forests and protects wildlife, but like the Sidhe and the Pooka, he has a dark and dangerous side. I have taken the liberty of making him the ruler of the Kinde Folke.

The next time you are in the woods, walk softly and speak quietly. Be alert to rustlings and scurrying in the underbrush. Take note of sudden flurries in the leaves at the tops of trees. Be aware of long-eared rabbits hiding in the ferns and sharp-eyed birds perched on branches. You never know how near the Kinde Folke may be, gliding silently through the woods in their cloaks of invisibility.

Should you meet such a one, do not believe a word she says. Accept no gifts. Be polite, but hurry on your way and do not look back.